J. F. Hoff D. D.
"OLNEY"
8 miles

HILL"

sberts

J. A. Shriver

W. C. Woods

Mrs. Delaughs

CHESTNUT SUMMIT

Road

Isaac Hartman

J a m e s · B o y c e

Mr. & Mrs. Thomas M. Keerl

NINTH DISTRICT

7 miles

PROPOSED

Est.

or.

Benj.

Bowen

SHEPPARD ASYLUM.

Moores

Chas.
isher

F. Pope

E. N. Sweeny

E. Pratt & Bro.

Mrs. Jas. Logue

H. C.
urnbull

H. C. Tur

MIDDLING PLANTERS OF
RUXTON
MARYLAND

MIDDLING PLANTERS OF
RUXTON
1694-1850

JOSEPH M. COALE III

MARYLAND HISTORICAL SOCIETY
BALTIMORE

MARYLAND
HISTORICAL SOCIETY
201 West Monument Street
Baltimore, Maryland 21201
Founded 1844

First Edition

Manufactured in the United States of America

ISBN 0-938420-56-9

LIBRARY OF CONGRESS CATALOGING-IN-PUBLICATION DATA

Coale, Joseph M.
   Middling planters of Ruxton, Maryland, 1694-1850
   Joseph M. Coale III. — 1st ed.
      p. cm.
   Includes bibliographical references (p. 77) and index.
   ISBN 0-938420-56-9 (alk. paper)
   1. Ruxton Region (Md.)—History.   I. Title.
F. 189.R89C63   1996
975.2'71—dc21
                                                96-47364
                                                CIP

To the memory
of
Jon F. Oster
and
Pierre J. Farley

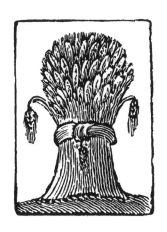

FRONTISPIECE:

The Ruxton White Oak, nearly 350 years old, stands on the east-west dividing line between the land grants, dating to 1694, of Young Man's Adventure and Samuel's Hope. Daily hundreds of drivers pass by the tree unaware of its antiquity. From its unique vantage point across Bellona Avenue from the St. John's AME Church, the oak has witnessed the evolving life of the Ruxton community, including operations of the Bellona Gunpowder Mills; the construction of the Baltimore & Susquehanna Railroad and a later disaster on that line; and the gradual transformation of this portion of the Roland Run Valley from wilderness to urban residential area. Abraham Lincoln passed here en route to Gettysburg. *(Maryland Bicentennial Commission Survey and Inventory, 1976, and Site Visit, Maryland Department of Natural Resources, State of Maryland, March 5, 1996.)*

Front endsheet map:

1. Detail from G. M. Hopkins, *Atlas of Baltimore Md. and Environs*, vol 2, plate R, 1877 (*Maryland State Archives, G 1213-453, 62-63.*)

Back endsheet map:

2. Detail from G. W. and W. S. Bromley, *Atlas of the City and County of Baltimore,* 1898. (*Maryland State Archives, G 1213-322.*)

Contents

—◆—

LIST OF ILLUSTRATIONS

LIST OF MAPS

Preface

———◦◦◆◦◦———

It is understandable that we so easily relate to national history because it is dynamic, visible, and well documented. To many people, local history seems routine, mundane, and unimportant; as a result it frequently is poorly recorded and soon lost. This is unfortunate, because the impact of local history on our lives as a catalyst for change is significant. Fortunately, the situation has improved in recent years. In scholarly quarters local history is more and more recognized as fertile ground for serious study. The rewards to those who pursue it are many.

My curiosity about Ruxton was aroused many years ago when I peeked through a shuttered window of the unused St. John's AME Church on Bellona Ave. Despite its Gothic Revival detailing, popular during the period of its construction in the 1880s, the church seemed a simple country chapel with plain board-and-batten siding and a rectangular shape. To this intruder, it was as if I were looking through the window of a time machine into the mid-nineteenth century. Undisturbed and complete with a pot-belly stove, old steel engravings of the Methodist circuit riders, oak pews and, a humble yet proud circular stained-glass window at the ceiling gable, the structure was an anachronism as traffic whizzed by to more contemporary destinations. With the adjacent unkept graveyard, there was an air of peace and solitude about the place that was both intriguing and inviting. I was caught by its charm and determined to unlock its secrets. At the time, no one seemed to know much about it or really seemed to care.

Although I knew little about local research methods, I was eager to see if any mysteries of this unique little building could be revealed. The study I was embarking on was not unlike a jigsaw puzzle. Three major land grants that made up the greater portion of the Ruxton area came together at a innocuous stone marker just outside the church's front door. During my subsequent search, each document, whether a deed, a will, an inventory, or other archival record, contained a clue about the culture and society from which it originated. Piecing the clues together in search of the larger picture was the challenge, and, with success, the satisfaction.

At the beginning, I pored over Towson Courthouse records looking for a history of ownership. Strange names began to appear with no indication or relevance to today's landscape. Those names took me to Baltimore City and then to Annapolis where most of the research was done. I found the thought of exploring a lost civilization captivating. Eighteenth- and nineteenth- century Baltimore County could not rival an Aztec or Roman exploration, but for me it was equally fascinating. Even those whose historic interest lies elsewhere will concede that the study of local history is convenient, relevant, and a cost-effective, hands-on experience.

St. John's was rescued several years later from, at best, an uncertain fate. After professional research, it was recorded in the National Register of Historic Places and restored through the efforts of a dedicated group of local preservationists and contributors and Governor Harry Hughes. A few yards to the east of the church rests the 350-year-old Ruxton Oak, which seems to guard St. John's while grudgingly accepting the intrusions of modern-day Bellona Avenue

This brief book is an effort to present the early history of a small but unique piece of Maryland, to show the relevance of that story to today, and to help prevent it from disappearing into oblivion.

I would like to recognize the late Jon F. Oster and the late Pierre J. Farley who showed me the workings of the Maryland Hall of Records and the Baltimore City and County Courthouses. Their friendship is greatly missed. The original and valuable research of John McGrain and George Horvath Jr., both distinguished Baltimore County historians, has contributed to this effort to increase the knowledge of our local heritage. I express my sincere appreciation and thanks to Dr. Edward C. Papenfuse, Maryland State Archivist; Dr. Jean Russo, Director of Research for the Historic Annapolis

Foundation; and Susan Cook and William Hollifield, independent researchers, for their help in critiquing my text. Any additional material that adds to the body of local knowledge about Ruxton will be welcome.

This book would not have been possible without the kind and generous support of the Maryland Historical Trust and its director, J. Rodney Little; Legg Mason; Philip and Lynn Rauch; and the Ruxton Village Apartments. I am grateful for their interest and enthusiasm for this effort.

J.M.C. III

Baltimore, Maryland

August 1996

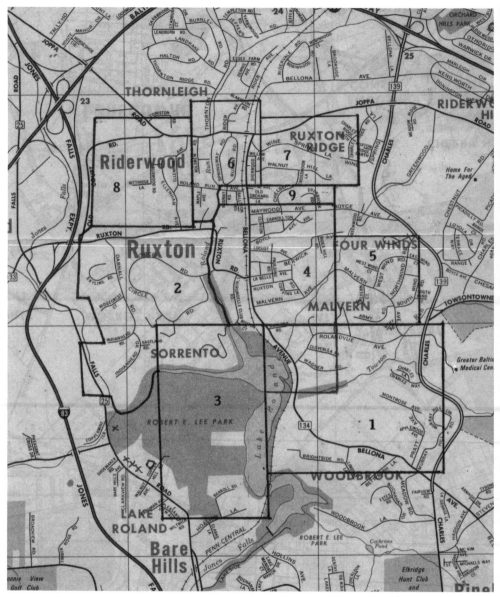

3. Ruxton land grants overlay. (*Collection of the author.*)

1. Samuel's Hope
2. Bosley's Adventure
3. Hector's Hopyard
4. Young Man's Adventure
5. Hooker's Prosperity
6. Martinton
7. Martin's Addition
8. Beale's Discovery
9. Coale's Good Luck

Introduction

—◦●◦—

Ruxton, Maryland recognized its three hundredth anniversary in 1994. Although known as Ruxton only for the last century, land in this portion of the Roland Run Valley, seven miles north of Baltimore City, was first granted by the Proprietor's land office in 1694. Maryland, with a population just shy of 35,000, was sixty years old at the time Ruxton began to be settled. This was the same year that the capital of Maryland moved from St. Mary's City to Annapolis. For its first two centuries, the area known today as Ruxton was identified by tract names, such as Samuel's Hope, Hector's Hopyard, Bosley's Adventure, Young Man's Adventure, Martinton, Hooker's Prosperity, and Beale's Discovery.

Compared with most other areas as close to the city, Ruxton has changed little over the intervening years. Its elevation on the fall line above the coastal plain has provided unique geological qualities that were recognized and valued from its earliest days of settlement. Rich natural resources of limestone, hardwood timber, soil, spring fed streams, excellent drainage, and ideal mill sites attracted settlers and provided opportunity.

Although for some time Ruxton courageously resisted acre by acre development, recent years have been especially harsh. Yet there are enough elements of rural character still preserved to suggest an earlier, less congested time.

Ruxton's history, in many ways, represents a microcosm of our country's transformation from wilderness to settlement, from agricultural to industrial, and from rural to urban. Both the causes and effects of these dynamic seventeenth- and eighteenth-century evo-

1

lutions that affected the entire colony, and indeed America, can be seen in this area's history. Surviving land records, chancery documents, estate wills and inventories, newspapers, probate petitions, and family records allow us to construct facts and reasonable hypotheses about the personalities that formed this community. By reconstructing the histories of the tracts that make up Ruxton and of those families who first settled here, we gain an understanding of the processes by which this region developed.

Access through this "perfect forest"[1] must have been an adventure in itself, especially for the first arrivals. During the early years of settlement most commerce, both export and import, probably traveled the course of the Old Court/Joppa Road. Originally a series of interconnecting Indian trails, and only more recently called Joppa Road, this was the primary east-west route to the back country from the tidewater. Founded by legislative action in 1707, Joppa served as the county seat and port of entry from 1712 until 1768, when by popular vote, both designations were removed to Baltimore. With the growth of the tobacco trade in the first half of the eighteenth century, the road became a rolling road, wide enough to roll hogsheads of tobacco across the county to Joppa for export.

A long ridge of land runs between the Jones Falls and Herring Run Valleys. In the early 1700s this was referred to as Little Britain Ridge. There, as north-south commerce slowly developed between the Patapsco River and southern Pennsylvania, a crude form of today's York Road started to take shape: the Britain Ridge Rolling Road. In the same period, Bellona Avenue, formerly Powder Mill Road, originated as a simple country lane to serve the planters and the mills that were established in the farming areas west of Britain Ridge in the Jones Falls and Roland Run Valleys.

To become a landowner, one had to receive land by bequest or apply for a grant from the Proprietor's land office. Grants could be obtained by buying land from an existing owner, by presenting oneself as a prospective farmer, or by paying the cost of passage of others into the colony (until 1683). Upon accepting the application, the land office issued a warrant, or an authorization for so many acres in a particular county. This warrant also recognized the name that the applicant wished to give his parcel of land. The county surveyor then laid out the desired property and issued a certificate of survey. Once

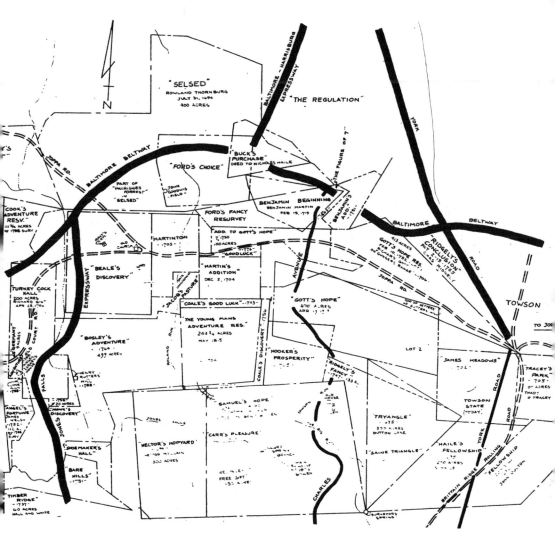

4. Ruxton-Riderwood map © 1979 by George J. Horwath. (*Maryland Historical Trust Survey BA 1559, 1979, by Dr. Arthur Tracy.*)

the survey was filed, a patent, or guarantee of ownership, secured the property for the landowner.

Study of the land records suggests that properties in Ruxton were settled by second- or even third-generation planters. For obvious reasons, land on the bay and along the rivers of the coastal plain in the northern Chesapeake was the most desirable and the first to be settled during the mid-to-late 1600s. These coastal and river landowners frequently held secondary inland tracts in the wilderness for trading and speculation and for the benefit of their descendants. These interior tracts were referred to as "quarters." Real estate and

3

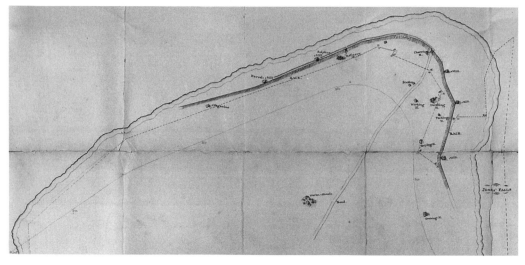

5. Bellona Gunpowder Mill plat. (*Maryland State Archives, Chancery L78 F146.*)

tobacco were the only widely held investment commodities at the time and full use of them was made as the economy developed.

While any attempt to generalize is risky, the early settlers in the Roland Run Valley largely belonged to the group commonly known as "middling" planters. On the economic and social scale, this group was situated between the small (often tenant) farmer and the aristocratic landed gentry. While analogies are weak, these planters were the rough equivalent of today's middle class. Over two-thirds owned land, as opposed to tenancy, with an average holding of about two hundred acres.

In 1719 only 15 percent of Maryland planters belonged to the middling group, with estates valued at death between one hundred and one thousand pounds sterling. Reflecting the growing wealth of the colony, that group had increased to 25 percent by 1739 and to 31 percent by 1759. Correspondingly, during these same years the number of estates valued at less than a hundred pounds was declining: 84 percent, 73 percent, and 67 percent, respectively. At no time during this period did more than 2 percent of estates exceed a thousand pounds. Despite these figures, many people have the false impression that the landed population consisted primarily of wealthy landed planters with magnificent estate houses.[2]

This account of early Ruxton draws heavily on two primary

6 . Detail from map of the City of Baltimore and Baltimore County by J. C. Sidney, 1850. (*Maryland State Archives, 1213-468.*)

CITY OF BALTIMORE

TOWSON TO

KELLYSVILLE

GOVENS

TOWS

HOME STEAD

Rail Road
County Road
County Road

W. Lowings
Charles Williams
W. Stevenson Saw Mill

H. H. Modell
Fred. Harrison

Brown
A. Brown

R. Jones

John Cooley's Tavern
J. G. Rider
S. C. Hunt

C. R. Taylor
E. C. Talbott

John Clarke
Rail Road

J. H. Price
J. Barton Criscum

J. Ridgely
J. Ridgely

John Ridgely

Mrs. Ford
8 Mile House Tavern
J. Burnett

W. & R. M. Lanahan
E. Norwood
J. Young Trustee

Jones's Walls

Browns Mills

Brown

Edwd Rider
Hunt Meeting ho

Edwd Rider
T. Burn

R. Jenkins

Epsom H.

N. H. Warr
Store

J. Keller

School

Mrs Jones

Dr W. Woods
Mrs Keller

J. Hiac

Mr Cole
C. Carroll

Edwd Rider
H. H. Ware

School ho
Richd Woods

R. Jenkins

H. Lechew
Epsom Chape
T. Witte

R. M. Dennison

O. P. Margitt
W. F. Johnson
Mrs Carroll

Dr W. Woods
Wm Tagart
Hoffman

G. W. McKenky

Lewis Roberts

Philip Poultney

D. J. Marsh
Amos Lushorn

P. W. Crees
W. H. Hammilton
J. W. Wesley

Edwd Taylor

J. H. Lloyd

C. R. Owings

S. Cole

Wm Althier

D. Lee

Colored Methodist ho

Philip Poultney

G. Dusum

R. N. Payne
R. N. Payne

J. E. Owen
Edwd Taylor
J. Parlet

J. Jackson

S. O. Cockey

Mrs Carroll

J. Ryost

Sam Hook

R. Hook

A. Barnham
F. Fispay
Bellona Powder ho

T. Ford

J. Bowen

R. Bowen

H. C. Turnbull

Edwd Sweeney

Edwd Stevens
Wm Hall

School
Church
Methodist Rector

Thos Flint
John M Hyse
Deer Park

J. Ritter

School ho
Penticola

W. C. Virgin

J. Beaty
Superintendt
Bare Hills

Yates
A. Scott
J. Hook

S. Barns

S. Armacost
Hatley House

Sam Pickering
Bellona
Powder Mills
Maguire

H. Y. Purviance

R. A. Taylor

R. A. Taylor

Oliver Merr
Saml. Harrison

W. Orndorff
Wm Orndorff

P. Robinson
Wm Well
Mrs Well
Joseph Smith
E. Wilson

R. Nevil
S. Gibbs
W. Wm Edge
R. Rond

C. M. Buchanan
Buckingham

W. C. Wilson

J. C. Harris

John Hopkins

R. A. Taylor

R. A. Taylor
T. Wildey

Ex. Myers

H. Taylor

D. S. Merceron

L. T. Williamson
Lexington

L. T. Williamson
James Beaty

L. T. Brien

D. S. Dorsey
John Glenn
John Glenn
Victor Sarata
Store

Jerome N. Bonaparte
Thos. Wildey
Academy

T. Wildey
Store

J. Trogler

J. W. Patterson

H. B. Atkins

F. Hamilton
A. E. Cox

G. W. Williamson

Beam

John Steel

G. C. Henricks

Saml Boon

J. Ward
Wm Stevenson

Springvale
W. C. Wilson

Miss Price
V. Dotan

C. Hall
J. Allison
Chan Whitney

J. W. Patterson
Isaac

J. B. Klunk
E. G. Kilborn

Anchorage
Rob. Wylie
Bland

T. Hook
Kitty Hook

Mrs Burk

A. Bradford

Mich Alder

J. H. T. Jerome

John Campbell

B. M. Perine

R. Hall
Store

E. Kernaut

T. Gate

Alfd Boyer
Saml Hill

Evans McHugh H.

Mrs Harper
C. Armat

D. Alder R. C. Church
Orphans Asylum

D. C. Rodger

Wm Roberts
G. Emanuel

H. Kirkpatrick

K. Hook

Rodgers

Mrs Tendall

Mrs Jews

McGovens
Store

TOWS
J. Burnes

W. Williams

A. Stir
J. Nicer

STOWN

TOOH

John Lewin
H. W. Nabb

Rural Mill
Flour
Ed Griffith

Mrs Mahon
Tavern

J. Baker
Store

Knight

Cold Spring Hotel

W. Smith

W. Smith
J. Shaw
Patterson

Crushers

Cap.
Merry Mill Lodge

J. Talbott

John Lewin
J. W. Ratcliffe
H. W. Nabb

J. P. Miller

J. P. Miller

J. M. Cornack
J. Gibson

Tonge

J. Tittle
J. E. Taylor
Kelly
Paradise Mill
J. Reed
T. Kenneth

R. Shaw
Patterson

Mrs Maxwell
Mrs Merryman

J. Gibson

C. Merryman
C. Hammett
J. Hammett
J. Taylor

Mrs Smith
Mrs Matkin

J. Printiss
Medfield
School

Jas Bay
Store

Denis Kelly
Store

KELLYSVILLE
H. Matkin

Saml Wymen

Mrs Dennett
James
Williams

Gibson
Stran

H. Leslie

J. S. Getting
Jacob Cox

Tavern
Wm Cusack

Butcher
C. Keyworth
R. Hammett

Thos Mathews
W. E. Hooper
Edwd Griffith
Tavern

Hoopers Woodberry
Factory

Ellicott
Heirs

White Hall
furn
Bap Church

J. Wilson

G. Rodgers
W. Wilson

R. Green

Dennett
H. Williams

Chesnut Hill

Homestead

Franklin Woollen Factory
Jordan

Ashland Factory

Mrs Bladford

J. Bell
Mrs Oram

L. Rodgers
Mrs Craft

W. Holmes
Mrs Giltmore

D. Ewing

Tiffany

Armstrong
Woollen Factory
Childs

A. Taylor
Little

Mrs Percy

J. M. Jordan

J. S. Gettings

Mrs Macaulay
T. T. Johnston
Mrs Boyle

L. Duncan

C. S. Gittings

Mrs Johnson
Mrs Greer

Dr T. Buckler

Brooks

Whitelock
Falknor

Davis

P. B. Sadler

J. Pearson
W. Williams

Bragg

R. Johnson

J. Stingluff
Beach Hill Forrest
Peck

T. Metherland

J. M. Lenth

J. Slodenbaker

J. Herry

John Stock
J. Kirby

Mount Hope

Green Mount
Cemetery
Chapel

Carpat.
Factory

John Merry
R. Johnson

Poplar Grove
Mrs House

Hrs R. Lyon

Methodist Chapel

Western
Cemetery

Levi Hoffman

S. Brown

CITY OF BALTIMORE

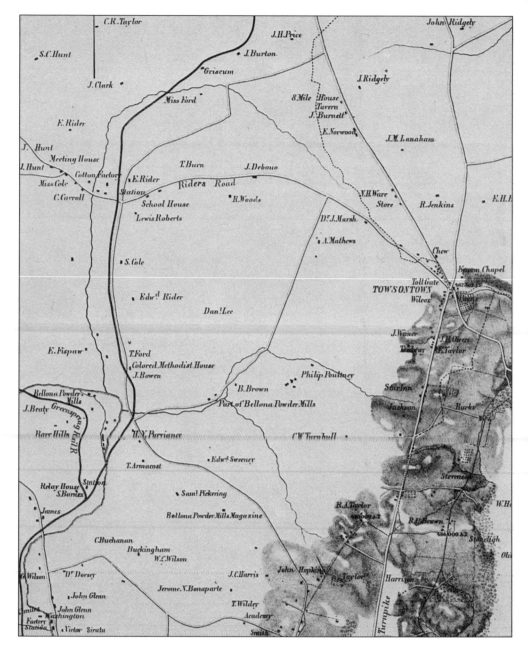

7. Detail from map of the City of Baltimore and Baltimore County by Thomas P. Chiffelle, 1852. (*Maryland State Archives, G 1213-264.*)

8. *Plan of Baltimore and Vicinity Showing the Proposed Routes for Bringing Water from the Jones Falls. . .* by James Slade, 1853. (*Courtesy Evergreen House, the Johns Hopkins University.*)

Brown

John Clarke

Miss Ford

Rocklandville
P.O. & Tavern

Edwd Rider

Edward Rider

Jesse Hunt

J. Hunt

Baltimore and Susquehannah Rail R.

School House

Wm Tagard

W. Tagart

S. Cole

Dr J

Rockland Print Works

G.W. McKankey

Amos T

ye Works

25 Feet above Tide

E. Fispaw

Proposed Works

Pla

B. Bowen

Bellona Powder Mills

Store

Bare Hill Tavern

Part of Bellona Powder Mills

Falls Turnpike

W. Tagart

Proposed Lake

H.V. Purriance

T. Armacost

J. Hook

119 Acres

Samuel Pickering

Bellona Powder Mills Maga
zine

R.A. Ta

R. Nevil
S. Gibbs
F. Welsh
B. Bond

S. Barne
Relay House

GAUGING

W.C. Wilson

C.M. Buchanan

Jones Beaty

Tunnel

G. Wilson

190

McEldery

Jerome N. Bonaparte

Academy

John

R.A

T

Victor Sirata

J. Ward

J.

Wm Stevenson

J. Frederick

V. Dolan

J.H.T. Jerome
C. Schelitt
J.M. Buchana
John (Burnl

Condui

Tunnel

J. Bradford

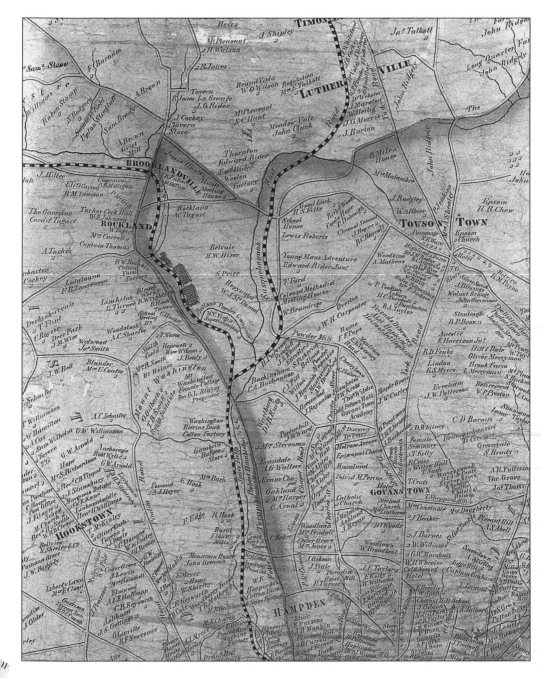

9. Detail from map of the City and County of Baltimore by Robert Taylor, 1857. (*Maryland State Archives, G 1213-470.*)

8

resource documents: the first Federal Census of 1790 and the Federal Assessment of 1798. From these, once the searcher is geographically oriented to the district names, a wealth of information is available about individuals, structures, properties, acreage, and wealth. For example, the 1790 population of the twenty households that resided in what is now Ruxton stood at approximately 236 and can be further broken down as follows: thirty-four free white males over sixteen and thirty-five under sixteen; sixty-one free females; and 106 slaves.

From these figures it is apparent that slaves were a definite factor in the planters' success. In Maryland as many families came to own slaves as owned land. As tobacco production increased, so did the demand for slaves; the number of Maryland planters owning slaves doubled between 1720 and 1760.[3] By the early nineteenth century, however, most slaves in the Roland Run Valley had been freed as a result of economic and religious pressures.

In the early 1700s, the first settlers of the Roland Run Valley initially cleared a few acres, constructed a temporary shelter, planted a subsistence crop of corn and a small cash crop of tobacco, and gradually established themselves as members of Maryland's planter society. Life was basic, yet over time it became adequate to comfortable, with more permanent, functional dwellings and necessary outbuildings serving the various agricultural requirements: spring houses, kitchens, barns, smoke houses, and sheds to store different crops and shelter animals. Generally, estates during the latter half of the eighteenth century were valued in the upper half of the middling range, between five hundred and a thousand pounds, and grew with each succeeding generation. Household chattels, tools, bedding, slaves, and even personal clothing were highly valued and often passed to heirs with specificity.

Since much material on Ruxton remains to be fully explored and analyzed, this history serves as a framework to stimulate further research.

The reader may wish to refer frequently to the maps on the endsheets of this book for orientation to the account that follows. There are no exact boundaries for Ruxton, but this sketch covers the general area bounded today by Charles Street on the east, Falls Road on the west, and Lake Roland and Joppa Road to the south and north.

Ruxton Chronology

1646	Ruxton White Oak, a seedling.
1694	First land grants laid out in Roland Run Valley.
1702	Earliest documented settlement (Hector's Hopyard).
1737	Forerunner of Bellona Avenue authorized by county court directive.
1743	Haile's Mill established on Roland Run at Joppa and Thornton Roads.
1764	Bosley's Adventure resurveyed at 499 acres; largest plantation under single ownership.
1767	Solomon Bowen Sr. home constructed, still standing on Greater Baltimore Medical Center property.
1773	First State Assessment of property owners.
1776	Livingston Academy established on Joppa Road.
1780	First Hunt Church constructed at present site.
1781	Robert Strawbridge, Methodist circuit preacher, dies on Hooker's Prosperity.
1790	First Federal Census – detailed local population statistics.
1795	Nicholas Ruxton Moore moves to his new home on Roland Run.
1798	First Federal Tax Assessment – property descriptions.
1801	Bellona Gunpowder Mills established at Roland Run and Jones Falls.
1814	Bellona Mills supplies 200 barrels of powder to Fort McHenry.
1816	Nicholas Ruxton Moore dies and is buried on the farm.
1820	Bellona Mills leveled by explosion.
1832	Legal conflict between Bellona Mills and property owners railroad over right-of-way.
1833	St. John's AME Church established.
1838	Baltimore & Susquehanna Railroad completed to York, Pennsylvania.
1854	First subdivision in area on Samuel's Hope (McDaniel lots).
1856	Great Ruxton train wreck; twenty-nine killed instantly.
1860	Lake Roland constructed.
1863	Lincoln travels through Ruxton by rail on way to Gettysburg Cemetery dedication.
1865	Lincoln funeral train passes on way to Harrisburg.
1877	Hopkin's Baltimore County Atlas published, showing details prior to urbanization.
1886	St. John's AME Church constructed, replacing original 1833 log cabin.
1887	Ruxton name used for first time to describe Circle Road development.
1894	Ruxton Heights development lots sold east of Bellona Avenue.

·1·

Samuel's Hope

Three of the seven land grants that comprise Ruxton originated from a two thousand-acre warrant issued by the Proprietor's land office to a certain Thomas Hooker of Baltimore County in 1694. Of these, "Samuel's Hope" at five hundred acres was the largest. The language used to lay out this perfectly rectangular grant has little reference to today's landscape. In the 1690s it was nearly as undisturbed as it had been at the time of America's discovery two centuries before.

The first call in the description of Samuel's Hope, "beginning at a white oak by a surveyor's spring," now lies a little to the northeast of the Bellona and Charles Street intersection. The grant continues "west 324 perches [a perch equals 16 1/2 feet] to a hickory," which placed the surveyor in the middle of what is now Lake Roland. Then "north 250 perches" to a point now a few yards northwest of the current Dunlop and Bellona Avenues. From there, due east for another 324 perches to the western edge of property formerly owned by the Sheppard Pratt Hospital and now the site of the Greater Baltimore Medical Center. The fourth and last call was "250 perches south to the beginning."[1] Thomas Hooker never lived on Samuel's Hope. Colonial records indicate that he was a land speculator who owned and traded much property in the county. His father, also a Thomas and a Quaker, had come to Maryland in 1649 as a result of the Act of Religious Toleration.[2]

The subdivision of Samuel's Hope began in 1716 when Hooker sold a hundred acres to Benjamin Carr for "15 pounds current money

11

of Great Britain."[3] Located in the northwestern portion of the property, this tract became known appropriately as "Carr's Pleasure." Two years later, Hooker granted 150 acres, the southwestern quarter known as the "Free Gift," to his son Samuel.[4] In 1720, Hooker sold the remaining eastern half of Samuel's Hope, consisting of 250 acres, to Benjamin Bowen.[5] Benjamin increased his holdings in Samuel's Hope to four hundred acres by purchasing Samuel Hooker's portion for seventy pounds sterling in 1736.[6]

In 1742 Benjamin Bowen Sr. died and bequeathed his various land holdings to his four sons: Benjamin Jr., Josiah, Nathan, and Solomon. From the will we learn that Benjamin Sr. had not taken residence on Samuel's Hope, but lived on a parcel called "Jonas' Cullot." Josiah was bequeathed this property and the "dwelling house" after the death of Benjamin's "beloved wife, Sarah." The other three sons who received shares of Samuel's Hope had already established residences on the property: Benjamin Jr., the southeastern portion, Nathan, the southwestern portion, and Solomon, the northeastern.[7]

The inventory of Benjamin Bowen Sr.'s estate lists separately every article he owned and its value. His household chattel for Jonas' Cullot contained over four pages of items from silk sheets to slaves. The legal purpose of inventories was to give public notice to creditors and beneficiaries for settling the estate, but today they provide an invaluable resource for depicting the amenities of daily life in mid-eighteenth-century Maryland. The total value of Bowen's personal estate was recorded as 853 pounds. Although still a middling planter, Bowen was considerably more comfortable than the average farmer of the period.

The most interesting element of this Bowen inventory was a separate listing for the "Quarter" (Samuel's Hope), a piece of land owned but not necessarily occupied. Such properties were usually held for speculation, rent, or for the future use of the owner's heirs. The property must have been settled prior to 1737 as the Baltimore County tax list for that year contains the entry, "at Benjamin Bowen's quarter, Ben Bowen Jr. two slaves."[8]

The origin and age of Bellona Avenue (Powder Mill Road) may well lie in the 1737 directive of the county court appointing Thomas Sheredine, road overseer, to lay out a road "from Hitchcock's Mill into the rolling road that goes down by Benjamin Bowen's quarter as the old road use[d] to go."[9]

The first son, Benjamin Jr., married his neighbor Mary Carr, daughter of Thomas and Elizabeth Carr, at Gunpowder Meeting in 1744.[10] When Benjamin Jr. died in 1770, Samuel Gott and Samuel Coale, neighbors who described themselves as Quakers, witnessed the will.[11] Benjamin, Jr. left an estate valued at 723 pounds of which his most valuable possession was a Negro male slave twenty years old valued at sixty-four pounds, one of twenty he owned. Benjamin Jr. also held an indenture on a white male servant named Thomas Wailer whose four remaining years of service were valued at seven pounds.[12]

Years later, in 1897, it was written of Benjamin Bowen Jr.:

> Of this pioneer nothing definite is known, but it may safely assumed that he was a man of excellent judgment and business sagacity for he selected for his home a place unsurpassed for fertility of soil and mildness of climate.[13]

Benjamin Jr. left his portion of Samuel's Hope to his son, Josias. Nine years later, in May 1779, Josias was recorded as being appointed a private in Captain Talbott's Company, one of the eight militia units organized in Baltimore County for the Revolution.[14]

The first Federal Census conducted in 1790 provides substantial detail of who was living in what was referred to then as the Back River-Upper Hundred area of Baltimore County. The census listed the head of each household by name and the number of persons in the household in five categories: free white males over sixteen, free white males under sixteen, free white females, all other free persons, and slaves. Josias appears as sole occupant of his household with five slaves.[15]

The Federal Direct Tax Assessment for the same area taken in 1798 shows Josias owning 150 acres of Samuel's Hope (plus 110 acres of the "Morgan's Delight" property to the south). In addition to the land, Josias owned six slaves, one old frame dwelling house 20 by 26 feet, one kitchen 16 by 18 feet, one stone smoke house 12 by 12 feet, one frame hen house 8 by 10 feet, and a stone barn 30 by 48 feet. The land was valued at $1,240 and improvements at $90.[16]

13

This early assessment record provides an invaluable research resource for developing a glimpse of the shape and extent of early Ruxton settlement nearly two hundred years ago. The document was a major undertaking for its day. It provides details for all properties, including names of the landowners, their farms, acreage, and slaves, as well as identifying buildings as to size, purpose, and construction. Today the assessment is extremely helpful in identifying the few remaining eighteenth-century structures.

Six years later, in 1804, the county assessment shows Josias with property valued at 764 pounds, considerably more than his brothers and nephews.[17] Note that on the Federal level dollars were properly used for evaluations in 1798, yet even as late as 1804 pounds were still the local standard. Old habits die hard.

Josias developed a prosperous working farm, but, according to the provisions of his father's will, if he died without "a lawfully begotten heir," his portion of the Samuel's Hope property would go to his younger brother, Thomas. This evidently happened for when Josias died in 1805 at the age of fifty-two, his will mentioned neither the property nor a wife and children. Earlier we noted that the Census of 1790 showed no other inhabitants of his household. However, he did provide for the "education and maintenance" of the children of Margaret George. Money raised from the sale of his personal property was to be invested in bank stock and held in trust for the support of children referred to as "Willis George or Bowen and Rebecca George or Bowen." The origin of this relationship is unclear. Josias's will also freed three of his eleven slaves and authorized monies earned from the bank stock to be used for their support. Others were to be freed when they reached the age of thirty-five, but until that time they were to be hired out and their wages used to buy bank stock. After being given freedom, stock earnings might be used for their support at the discretion of the executor. A self-funding trust instrument was thus established.[18]

Josias's brother Thomas Bowen held the property until 1818 when he returned to Baltimore from his residence in North Carolina to sell his inherited southeastern third (168 acres) of Samuel's Hope and family home to Edward Buchanan of Baltimore City for $8,248.[19] Buchanan's estate sold the farm in 1844 to Edward N. Sweeney, who later appears on the Sidney and Chiffelle maps (*see maps 6 and 7*).

The original residence, built by Benjamin Bowen Jr., stood on a site north of Bellona Avenue and west of Applewood Lane, adjacent to the source of the Negro Spring Branch that leads down to the Great Run. This small tributary remains active today and is identified on both the Hopkins and Bromley maps (*see front and back endsheets*).

Benjamin Sr.'s son, Nathan, lived on the tract called the "Free Gift" and established a successful plantation there as evidenced by his will probated December 5, 1770.[20] His inventory included seven slaves, twenty-one sheep, five horses, four head of cattle, three hogs, and numerous other articles for a value of 369 pounds.[21] Three years later, in the first recorded tax census of Back River-Upper Hundred, "Mary, widow of Nathan Bowen" was listed as head of the household.[22] The farm passed to Nathan Jr., who is shown in the Federal Assessment of 1798 with a dwelling house valued at $50, six slaves, and 148 acres of Samuel's Hope. Nathan Jr. died in 1810 and willed the farm to his son Charles.[23] Nathan Jr.'s inventory also revealed a bountiful and successful farming operation for his period. Over five pages of farm equipment, live stock, household goods, carpenter tools, and food stocks are described. He owned twelve slaves, all but two of whom were under sixteen years of age. Nathan left seven hundred gallons of cider, thirty-three barrels of corn, twenty bushels of rye, twenty-five bushels of wheat, twenty-one sheep, seven horses, six fat hogs, etc. etc. His total inventory (excluding real property) was valued at $3,454.47 – a considerable holding.[24]

After nearly a hundred years and four generations of Bowen ownership, Charles sold his inherited 153 acres of Samuel's Hope to Hoop Chamberlin in 1816.[25] As did others in the Roland Run Valley, Hoop later lost property (5.6 acres) to the Baltimore & Susquehanna Railroad in 1828 in a condemnation process.

Solomon, the fourth son of Benjamin Sr., inherited the northeastern portion of Samuel's Hope. In 1752, ten years after his father's death, referring to himself in the deed as a planter, he had purchased the adjacent hundred acres known as Carr's Pleasure from Thomas Carr, a blacksmith, for fifty pounds.[26] Judging from the three-fold increase in the value of the property from when it was purchased thirty-six years before, Carr had established a successful farm and blacksmith operation. Solomon now enjoyed ownership of the northern half of Samuel's Hope consisting of 224 acres.

Thus, by 1752, the entire five hundred-acre tract known as Samuel's Hope was under Bowen ownership with Solomon owning, approximately, the northern half, Benjamin Jr. the southeastern quarter, and Nathan the southwestern quarter. All had established farms and permanent dwellings on these parcels.

For the next hundred years the Carr's Pleasure portion of Samuel's Hope remained in the Bowen family. During the early eighteenth century Solomon Sr. and Jr. are shown frequently in various routine legal documents pertaining to the daily life of the area: recording deeds, witnessing wills, assessing estate inventories, etc. In 1768 both participated in the election to move the county seat from Joppa to Baltimore. The Assessment of 1773 lists Solomon Sr. and Jr. The Federal Census of 1790 records both but now separately, as heads of households, indicating that the latter had taken up residence on the Carr's Pleasure site.

The Back River-Upper Hundred listing for the Federal Direct Tax Assessment of 1798 shows Solomon Sr. with a 126-acre farm, an old frame dwelling house 20 by 34 feet, a log kitchen 18 by 24 feet, a meat house 8 by 10 feet, a frame stable 14 by 20 feet, an old frame barn "fit for fuel" and a stone mill house. In this first Federal assessment, the owner had the unique advantage of setting the evaluation himself, which Solomon Sr. did at $504 for land and $70 for improvements. Solomon Jr. was listed at $393 with ninety-eight acres of Samuel's Hope (Carr's Pleasure) although he did not acquire formal title until 1804 when his father died and bequeathed the property to him: "All that part of a tract called Samuel's Hope whereon he now resides which was bought of Thomas Carr."[27]

Solomon's home, "where I now dwell," was left to his son Benjamin. This home, originally constructed by Solomon Sr., still stands, although in a much neglected state, on the high bluff of the Greater Baltimore Medical Center property overlooking the southeast corner of Charles Street and Towsontown Boulevard. The chimney is proudly inscribed with a 1767 construction date. Regrettably, this artifact now serves as a storage and maintenance shed that hardly acknowledges the respect it is due, being older than the Republic itself.

Sometime prior to 1798, Solomon Bowen, Sr. had also constructed a stone mill house and millrace on a two-acre site on the north side of the Great Run.[28] This area today is about a quarter-mile west of Charles Street between Malvern Avenue and Charles Way. As mentioned, the Assessment of 1798 that detailed the various structures of Solomon's 126-acre farm, included "a stone mill house." At his death in 1804, Solomon Sr. willed the mill to sons Josias, William, and Elijah as joint tenants. In 1811 the latter two released their interests in the mill to Josias, and he became the sole owner and proprietor. For some time prior to this transaction, he was recorded as a "miller." The mill was eventually sold with the surrounding land to the Bellona Gunpowder Company and used as a storage building, after which the structure was abandoned. Its humble foundations and millrace quietly remain in the woods today with little in the immediate vicinity having changed in nearly two centuries. The site appears on the 1852 Chiffelle Baltimore County map.(*See map* 7).

The Assessment of 1804 reveals quite a difference in evaluation of Solomon Jr.'s property, now at 315 pounds, and Sr.'s at seventy nine pounds. Solomon Sr. had likely died by this time, but his estate probably had not been settled and thus was still carried by the assessment.

Over the next thirty years, Solomon Jr. further developed the successful plantation left to him by his father. However, we do not know many details of his daily life during this period of the early nineteenth century. He was not pressed into service during the defense of Baltimore in the War of 1812 as were his cousins and neighbors, Benjamin C. Bowen and Thomas W. Bowen. Both distinguished themselves as privates serving under Lieutenant Colonel Nicholas Ruxton Moore, commander of the Baltimore County 6th Cavalry District.[29] Certainly the frequent explosions (no fewer than five) across Jones Falls at the Bellona Gunpowder Mills and the resulting loss of property and human life must have been alarming.[30] However, the arrival of the railroad, in 1832, through what had been his front yard, must have been even more disturbing. After a condemnation process which Solomon fought strongly, as did his neighbors, the Baltimore & Susquehanna Railroad confiscated over three acres of his farm, and an impartial jury awarded no damages to Solomon.[31] The following year he died.

In his will there is no mention of his children, who were perhaps deceased or strongly out of favor, but only his seven grandchildren.

The granddaughters received $150 each, while the grandsons were bequeathed the real estate or the value thereof if sold upon reaching the age of twenty-one. The executors were directed to provide sufficient clothing and board for the beneficiaries.[32]

The 1834 inventory of Solomon's estate was witnessed by Edward Rider, a neighbor of considerable local stature who was acting in his official capacity as a justice of the peace for the county. A few items and their appraised value from the inventory list that totals $1,013.50 are of interest:

> 4 turkies 4.00
> 500 lbs.bacon 40.00 (in cellar)
> 15 cords of wood 15.00
> 2 old guns 10.00
> 1 field of rye 6.00 (near railroad)
> 1 buffalo bull 15.00 [33]

In her eighteenth year as a widow, Solomon Jr.'s wife, Jemina, sold Carr's Pleasure to a Thomas Lanahan in October 1852.[34] In August of that year, an advertisement had appeared in the *Baltimore County Advocate* giving us a glimpse of what was offered. Many attractive selling points were noted, among them:

> 134 acres of prime land in a fine state of cultivation, having been improved by the application of 150 bushels of lime per acre a few years past which had greatly invigorated the soil. A good orchard of good fruit well watered by several fine springs . . . streams running through every field . . . acres of woodland . . . a dwelling house porches on both sides . . . a new barn 60 x 40 feet . . . a stone stable with loft that holds 15 tons of hay, a new corn house, two dairies, blacksmith shop, cider house and hay barracks; two lime kilns that will burn 1,300 bushels each with prime quality lime 100 yards from the kiln.[35]

Despite earlier problems with the railroad and the powder mill, Carr's Pleasure was nearly self-supporting and obviously a prosperous country residence. Purchased by Thomas Lanahan for $12,000, the property was held for only one year before being sold for the same price to John L. Reese of Baltimore City in 1853. Later the same year, Carr's Pleasure again changed hands when James McDaniel bought the property from Reese.[36]

Portions of Samuel Bowen's residence possibly predate 1752, when he purchased a hundred-acre portion of Samuel's Hope from Thomas Carr, a blacksmith. *(Collection of the author.)*

It was more than just a coincidence that property formerly held in one name for more than a century could experience three transfers within one year. There is a simple explanation. With the proposed construction of Lake Roland to supply the needs of an ever-growing Baltimore and the railroad providing efficient access, the property came under increasing development pressure. Over the next ten years McDaniel subdivided his property into eight lots (including a thirty-seven-acre parcel condemned for Lake Roland) ranging in size from two to forty acres.[37]

The home of Solomon Bowen Jr., originally built by the Carrs and much added to over the years, still stands on the west side of Bellona Avenue between Dunlora and Rolandvue Roads. Thomas Brundridge bought this thirteen-acre parcel from McDaniel in 1857.[38] Giant oaks and aged boxwoods surround the residence as if in respectful vigilance over the dwelling's 250-year-old existence. Although impossible to date precisely, a recent site survey performed by the Maryland Historical Trust "points strongly toward a pre-1776 construction date" for at least a portion of the house.[39] Bowens who resided in the house over the years have etched their initials in the window panes on the first floor of this proud home.

Great value was added to the Bowen properties in 1857 when Charles Street was extended from Merryman's Lane (University Parkway) to Powder Mill Road (Bellona Avenue.) despite local opposition. This new access direct to Baltimore City and the development of Lake Roland were major catalysts for accelerated development during this period.[40]

As mentioned earlier, Solomon Jr.'s brother, Benjamin, inherited the family residence and the northeastern section of Samuel's Hope. Although Benjamin's will cannot be located, the property was in turn left to his son, also Benjamin, who died in 1877. He had no children and the property "inherited from our father and where we have lived all our lives" eventually passed to his brother William's son, George V. Bowen.[41] George died in 1897 but the property continued to be held in his estate as late as 1906 and is shown on the Bromley map of 1998 *(see back endsheet)*. Shortly, the last parcels of Samuel's Hope passed out of Bowen hands after nearly two centuries of ownership.[42]

The earliest cartographic history in any detail of Samuel's Hope and of Ruxton is the J. C. Sidney Baltimore County map of 1850 *(see map 6)*. It shows the home of "B. Bowen" to the east and "J. Bowen" (Jemina, Solomon's widow) on the Carr's Pleasure portion at the western side of the property. On the Chiffelle map, as amended by Slade in 1853 *(see map 8)*, stream valleys of the entire area are shown topographically as possible city reservoir sites. Also detailed are the courses of a country road that roughly paralleled the Great Run (Towson Branch) as it cut diagonally across the Samuel Hope property.[43] In early source material, this still picturesque stream was also referred to as Bowen's Run. The country road later became the pro-posed right-of-way for a Towsontown rail spur, shown on the Hopkins' map of 1877 *(see front endsheet)* but never completed. Running from where Bellona Avenue crosses the Great Run north-east up the stream valley, its roadbed can still be seen emerging from the woods on the west side of the Charles Street and Towsontown Boulevard intersection. From there it followed the current course of Charles Street Avenue to Joppa Road.

The Chiffelle and Slade maps also record the right of way of the Baltimore & Susquehanna Railroad as it crossed and recrossed Powder Mill Road (Bellona Avenue), first at the bottom of the hill from Charles Street and again in front of J. Bowen's home. Bellona was realigned to the east side of the railroad when Lake Roland was constructed. Two of the Bellona Gunpowder storage magazines are identified on these maps, as well, one on the site of the Bowen mill and the other on the south side of Bellona Avenue just west of Charles Street.

21

·2·

Hector's Hopyard

———————◆◆◆———————

To the west of Samuel's Hope lies the three-hundred acre grant known as Hector's Hopyard. This parcel played host to a variety of events unequaled in any other tract in this survey. Though only the northern section actually lies in our area of study, our coverage of this grant is appropriate because of its long association with the Ruxton community. Accommodating at various times from its first settlement a hops and tobacco farm, a grain mill, a gunpowder factory, a copper ore mine, a railroad, and a water reservoir, the Hopyard has been home to an extraordinary range of uses over the past three hundred years.

The history of the Hopyard has been strongly influenced by a unique geological resource. A large outcropping of metamorphic serpentine rock containing chromium and copper ore permeates most of the property. In addition to being commercially mined for its metal content, this greenish rock has long been used also as a local source of building material and ornamentation. The ore was initially discovered on the adjacent Bare Hills property by Isaac Tyson in 1811. Isaac's father, Jesse, a wealthy merchant, helped finance his son's early career that led to his becoming one of Baltimore's most successful industrialists.

Along with Samuel's Hope and Young Man's Adventure to the east, the Hopyard originated from the Thomas Hooker warrant of 1694 for 2,000 acres. Hooker assigned half of this warrant to James Murray who in turn passed the acreage to Hector McClane for his hopyard.[1] Logically we can assume its initial or intended purpose was for the cultivation of hops.

The first call in the description of Hector's Hopyard starts "at a red oak on the east side of the northeast branch of Jones Falls." The

23

red oak has long since disappeared, but there is a boundary stone that marks its former location just outside the door of the St. John's AME Chapel on Bellona Avenue across from Dunlora Road. This stone also serves as the extreme northwest corner of Samuel's Hope. The Hopyard runs due west from this point 150 perches (one-half mile) across the Roland Run bridge on Club Road and along a white picket fence toward Falls Road. The second call is due south 350 perches, then east 150 perches, and north to the beginning. This last call adjoins the westernmost line of Samuel's Hope. The area includes a portion of Bare Hills and the junction of the Jones Falls and Roland Run streams before the construction of Lake Roland.

McClane evidently took up residence shortly after acquiring title. When he sold the northern two hundred acres of the Hopyard to James Carroll of Anne Arundel County in 1702, the deed stated that McClane was a planter and that the farm was being sold with "orchards, fences and improvements."[2] This is the earliest documentation of Ruxton settlement.

At his death in 1729, Carroll bequeathed his two hundred acres of the Hopyard equally between his cousin Edward Tully and the two sons of his cousin Michael Tully.[3] In 1742, the latter sold their portion for sixty pounds to Edward Tully's son-in-law, Jacob Young, who had married Tully's daughter Eleanor.[4]

In 1746, Jacob Young received a fifty-acre grant, adjoining the southern boundary of the Hopyard, known as Young's Delight.[5] When the property was resurveyed in 1750, he was also granted 175 acres of adjoining vacant property all to be held in the name of Young's Delight. This brought his total holdings to 325 acres.[6]

The Youngs lived either on Eleanor's father's portion of the Hopyard or neighboring Young's Delight. Soon after Jacob acquired his cousins' acreage, portions of their original holdings were sold off: nineteen acres to John Bosley of Bosley's Adventure (1749), a hundred acres to Ann Fishpaw (1751), and sixteen acres to John Fishpaw (1769).[7] All three of these properties were north of Jones Falls, which travels west to east across the upper third of the Hopyard. The falls also served conveniently to divide the Hopyard between the Back River-Upper Hundred district on the north, and the Middlesex Hundred district to the south (as these portions of Baltimore County were called prior to 1789).

Jacob Young and Edward Tully both died in 1782. Tully granted his daughter Eleanor a life estate in his property but willed his hundred acres to his grandson, Michael Young. Jacob left an estate valued at 722 pounds, placing him in the upper middling range.[8]

The Assessment of 1783 confirms that the approximate northern third of the Hopyard (north of Jones Falls) was held by John Fishpaw (116 acres) in the Back River-Upper Hundred district.[9] The property is again reflected in the Federal Assessment of 1798, where it was listed with two frame dwelling houses 20 by 28 feet and 16 by 20 feet, two log outhouses 10 by 12 feet each, two stables, one log and the other frame, 14 by 16 feet and 22 by 32 feet, respectively, on 114 acres.[10]

In 1783, Eleanor Young was shown with a hundred acres and her three children with thirty-three acres each, in the Middlesex district. Jacob, though deceased, is nevertheless recorded with fifty acres of Young's Delight. In the Federal Census of 1790, Eleanor was listed as head of a family, with one male over sixteen (Michael), three white females, and five slaves.[11] She died in 1808.[12] However, by 1798 Michael was recorded as owning numerous structures, 250 acres in Middlesex Hundred and six slaves, all in the Hopyard, as a result of the legacy left by Eleanor's father and husband.

The impact of the Industrial Revolution came to the Roland Run Valley with a real bang in 1801 when property was acquired that led to the establishment of the Bellona Gunpowder Company. In March of that year, for "560 pounds current money of the United States," in the first of a series of sales Michael Young sold fourteen acres along Jones Falls to several local merchants – Alexander McDonald, Nicholas G. Ridgely, and Noah Nelms. They were granted "free and uninterrupted quantity and enjoyment of the Millrace until it empties into the Falls."[13] Other transfers occurred from the Young family to the Bellona Gunpowder Company in 1803, 1817, and 1819. In 1827, Young's estate transferred the largest parcel, 196 acres, for $10 per acre. This last acreage was described as "not susceptible of much cultivation and yet is exceedingly valuable from the quantity of chrome with which it abounds."[14] Fishpaw had also sold several parcels along the Falls to the Powder mills, granting permission for the millrace and dam.[15]

Dying intestate in 1818, Michael still owned 224 acres of the

Hopyard and adjoining land named Young's Delight.[16] However, the family graveyard was located within the Hopyard proper at the southwestern side of the junction of Jones Falls and Roland Run. Remnants remained until recent years.

Returning our attention to the second parcel of the Hopyard, the hundred-acre southern portion was reacquired by James Murray in an exchange (1698) with Hector McClane for another Baltimore County property of equal size, Hunting Ridge.[17] A series of transfers followed, beginning in 1704 when the property was willed to Murray's five-year-old son Jabus (1699-1761) who later married Mary Wheeler, the daughter of William and Martha Wheeler of Hooker's Prosperity, located to the east.[18] At Jabus's death, his son, William, sold the property for twelve pounds to cousins McClane and Jabus Bailey.[19] The parcel was held by Jabus Bailey until his death in 1769 when it was willed to his nephew, Joseph Bailey.[20] John Cockey acquired the farm for 900 pounds and some unspecified additional "costs and charges" in 1779 and promptly sold it the same year for 6,000 pounds to William Smith.[21] It is unclear what this contingency represented although it must have been significant.

Twenty years later Smith sold the farm to Josias Bowen (see Samuel's Hope).[22] Bowen died in 1811 and the property was advertised for public auction in the *Baltimore American*:

FARM AND MILL SEAT KNOWN
BY THE NAME OF HECTOR'S
HOPYARD — 100 ACRES OF LAND
.... A HANDSOME FARM[23]

The following year, this portion of Hector's Hopyard was purchased by Charles Ridgely of Hampton[24] and later transferred by deed of gift to his son, Charles Jr., in 1818.[25]

John Fishpaw lived on his northern portion of the Hopyard until his death in 1825, when the farm passed to his son, Elijah.[26] Both father, as a major, and son, as a sergeant, served in the War of 1812 in the Maryland Militia in the defense of Baltimore. As a result of Elijah's four months' service, his widow at the age of eighty-one in 1860 applied for and was awarded a 120-acre grant for western land under the Bounty Land Act of 1855.[27]

26

St. John's AME Church was established in 1832 when the railroad right-of-way cut off the extreme northeastern quarter-acre of Hector's Hopyard. The original church, a simple log cabin, was replaced by the present-day Gothic revival structure in 1886. St. John's is now listed on the National Register of Historic Places. *(Collection of the author.)*

During the Fishpaw ownership, a few lots were sold off, but the most interesting transaction occurred on October 28, 1833. Elijah Fishpaw, for $15 in "good and lawful money of the United States of North America," sold to several freed slaves a site currently on the west side of Bellona Avenue just northwest of the present Dunlora Road for a church and graveyard. The trustees of the church, described as "descendants from Africa," were sold the land with the restriction that it was to be used solely as a burying ground and a meeting house. If ever used for any other purpose, the property was to revert back to Fishpaw or his descendants.

The parcel had been created in 1832 when construction of the Baltimore & Susquehanna Railroad cut off the extreme northeastern corner (¹/₄ acre) of Hector's Hopyard from the main body of the prop-erty.[28] The first church had been a log cabin, but in 1886 the present structure was completed. Originally referred to as the Bethel Episcopal Methodist Religious Society in the deed of conveyance, the cornerstone of the present structure names it St. John's AME Church. The site is identified on historic maps, which show the orig-inal course of Bellona Avenue to be on the west side of the church.

Elijah died in 1854 at age seventy-three. In the following year his children sold their 104 acres of the Hopyard to James McDaniel for $7,315.[29] McDaniel apparently speculated on the Lake Roland project and had also purchased the adjacent Carr's Pleasure, a portion of Samuel's Hope. Taking a loss on the Hopyard property, he sold it to James and Hugh Warden the following year for $5,520.[30] After the Baltimore City government condemned thirty-seven acres for the Lake Roland project,[31] the Wardens' remaining property was subdi-vided (1866) into two country estates of thirty-five and thirty-one acres where handsome residences were soon constructed and remain today.[32] These homes, in addition to the farm formerly held by Nicholas Ruxton Moore to the north, were served by a road that ran directly from Bellona Avenue along the north side of St. John's Church to the current Club Road bridge over Roland Run. Its roadbed is still visible. In the cartographical record only the 1857 map by Robert Taylor still honors two of the original land grant names, the Hopyard and Young Man's Adventure. (*See map 9.*)

The Bellona Gunpowder Works

As we have seen, the area owned by the Tully, Young, and Fishpaw families became the site of the Bellona Gunpowder Company of Maryland.

In 1774, although the English proprietary government still existed in name, the Maryland Provincial Convention became the state's administrative, planning, and organizing arm for the coming war with Great Britain. Measures were taken to assist the people of Massachusetts against General Thomas Gage's forces, as well as to prepare Maryland itself against possible encroachment from what was fast becoming the enemy. On July 26 of the following year, the Convention authorized formation of Committees of Observation

The du Pont factories at
Brandywine, Delaware, *(at left)*
competed with the Bellona
Mills *(below)* in the 1820s and
1830s. This structure at du
Pont was typical of those used
for gunpowder production:
three thick stone walls with
the fourth side open so explosions, a constant hazard, would
be directed away from adjacent
buildings.
*(Courtesy Hagley Museum,
Wilmington, Delaware.)*

which "were to have full power and authority to carry into execution the resolves of the Continental Congress and the Conventions of this province."[33]

Appointed chairman of the Baltimore Committee of Observation was a distinguished local merchant, Samuel Purviance. By December 1775, the Committee addressed the need for Baltimore to have a self-sufficient supply of high quality gunpowder. Accordingly, provision was made for a facility to be built not more that fourteen miles or less than six miles from the city.[34] The Hopyard location met all requirements. The mill was to be seven miles from the city at the junction of Jones Falls and Roland Run, there was an ample supply of fresh water complete with a constructed millrace and power from it, the area was isolated yet a good road gave access (Falls Road), and the mill was on the northern side of the city. An enemy was most likely to approach from the south and the Chesapeake Bay or its tributaries.

Given the volatile nature of the product, the Bellona Mills – named for the Roman goddess of war – were soon besieged by a series of accidental explosions. The first occurred in November 1801. Though it killed no one, it completely destroyed one 30 x 40-foot mill house and "every atom in it." A more serious calamity occurred in 1812 when a saltpeter shed caught fire and spread to four adjoining structures causing violent explosions and destruction.[35]

Despite such setbacks, by December 1814 the Bellona Mills had grown to such a degree as to make incorporation desirable. The General Assembly passed an act to that effect and the name officially became The Bellona Gunpowder Company of Maryland.[36] Prior to this time, all obligations and commitments the company made were in the names of its various owners: Noah Nelms, Nathan and Peter Levering, Enoch and Jesse Levering, Alexander McDonald, Nicholas G. Ridgely, and James Beatty.

James Beatty eventually became sole owner and operator and by 1815 had secured an indirect compliment from competitor E.I. du Pont: "One of our principal motives is to strive against the competition of the Baltimore markets."[37]

Since military stores were largely locally supplied, it is not surprising that the gunpowder "warranted to be fully equal to any at market" produced at the Bellona Mills was used to repel the British attack on Fort McHenry and North Point. In a letter dated June 12, 1814, the chief ordinance officer of the U.S. War Department, Decius Wadsworth, ordered James Calhoun of the local Federal Commissary to purchase two hundred barrels of gunpowder from the Bellona Works to be placed in the magazine at Fort McHenry.[38]

Only a small portion of the Hopyard acreage along the Jones Falls was actually used for the manufacturing process. The remainder was later mined for its chrome and cooper ore and used for scattered storage of the finished product awaiting shipment. As the mills developed, the operation grew to occupy 350 acres at its zenith, employed nearly fifty workers, and produced one-fifth of the powder for the American civilian and military markets.[39]

Misfortune again struck in August 1820 when the works were shattered by the most serious explosion ever suffered, reportedly heard as far away as Washington and Chestertown. Three workers were instantly killed; one victim was described as having been blown four hundred yards with the loss of his head, legs, one arm, and entrails. According to the *American Commercial and Daily Adviser*:

> Between 9 and 10 yesterday morning two distinct explosions were heard in this city accompanied by concussions such as have been experienced after the blowing up of the Powder Mills. The appearance of an immense volume of smoke in the direction of the Bellona Powder Works left little or no doubt of what had taken place, and excited much anxiety for the fate of the men employed in the works.[40]

How Mr. Beatty ever recovered from the "scene of awful and utter destruction" is unclear. Requiring a profit of 10 percent to cover losses occasioned by accidental explosions, Beatty thought of closing down because his profit margin failed to exceed 3 percent.[41] Yet even with additional explosions in 1821 and 1830 and increasing competition from the du Pont factories the Bellona Gunpowder Mills managed to stay in business. There can be no doubt that these problems had an exhausting effect on Beatty's credit and must have taken him a number of times to the edge of bankruptcy.

While struggling to stay in business, Beatty watched with great concern the encroachment of the Greenspring Branch of the Baltimore & Susquehanna Railroad. The road was to pass through his property on its way to Westminster, following the western bank of the Jones Falls. This would turn a business already dangerous by nature into one bordering on suicide. Early locomotives were known for the fire hazards of sparks and smoke. The first route proposed by the Railroad in 1830 was not especially objectionable to the company as it was to pass far enough to the west of the mill works to permit a comfortable margin of safety. At the last moment, however, plans were changed; the new route came much closer to the buildings and so seriously compromised the safety of the workers and the operation that it would have been forced to shut down or move.

In a bill of complaint filed on August 5, 1831, the company's lawyers requested the court to compel the railroad to use the route first proposed. It was argued that moving the mill works would be economically unfeasible as from $70,000 to $80,000 had been invested in buildings and other construction. In addition, $23,000 of raw materials had already been stockpiled for the ensuing season. The primary legal argument, however, was that the railroad did not have the power of condemnation over another corporation; this power only applied to individually owned properties. Further, the Bellona Gunpowder Company had been incorporated in 1814 long before the railroad and as a result should have preemptive rights.[42]

A colored site plat filed by the company showed the route of the proposed railroad and detailed the different structures of the gunpowder mills. These included the barrel and sulfur mills, the refinery, the charring mills, and the superintendent's residence, all shown along the millrace and Jones Falls. (*See map 5*). A second, crudely drawn map of the site in the late 1830s is in the collection of the Hagley Museum and Library in Wilmington, Delaware. Unidentified until compared with the railroad plat, this second map indicates the du Pont firm's interest in the Bellona Gunpowder Company site. Whether the purpose of the second map was simply to obtain knowledge of the competition or to prepare for a future acquisition we cannot know, but it appears to be an early case of industrial espionage.[43] The map was made by a representative of du Pont, with notations of "unknown lands" and mislabeled roads.

Various depositions were entered by workers and experts as evidence that expounded on the very real dangers to be encountered from the intrusion of the railroad. The fire hazard inherent in early locomotives was feared not only by farmers but especially by those engaged in the manufacture of such a delicate commodity as gunpowder. From the bill of complaint: "Such is the nature of the said manufacturing and the hazard of carrying on the same that workmen cannot be procured to carry it on if subjected to the increased hazard and consequence upon such a thoroughfare as a public road."

The judicial outcome, favorable to Beatty, awarded him $1,200 for the 7¼ acres taken and required the railroad to use the first proposed right-of-way through the property.[44]

The Census of 1850 records James Beatty as eighty years of age and living in Baltimore City with his wife Elizabeth, seventy-five. Beatty's death was noted in October of the following year by the *Baltimore Sun*: "During his long life he sustained a character which combines the most exalted traits and was also a most honorable citizen in all relations of life."[45]

After his father's death, Beatty's son Charles carried on the business until 1853 when a large portion of the property was sold to Baltimore City for its new water works and the consideration of $17,500.[46] Afterward, Charles Beatty continued the powder business at the Battleworks on the Liberty Turnpike until 1867 when he sold out because of increasing costs and competition.[47] Ruins of the Bellona Gunpowder Mills were standing as late as 1911 but were soon covered by silt removed from Lake Roland. The millrace is still prominent on the site, but few could identify its historic origin or purpose. Its dry bed is now used exclusively for dirt biking.

This white fence at L'Hirondelle Club Road and Roland Run marks the north-south property line between Hector's Hopyard and Bosley's Adventure. An early 1800s graveyard was located here, possibly the site of Nicholas Ruxton Moore's final resting place. *(Photo collection of the author)*

·3·

Bosley's Adventure

———————

To the north of Hector's Hopyard and west of Young Man's Adventure, lies the 499-acre tract known as Bosley's Adventure. In 1795, from a part of this grant, Ruxton's most illustrious patriot, soldier, politician, and farmer, Colonel Nicholas Ruxton Moore, purchased his plantation of 350 acres. Bosley's Adventure today roughly borders Roland Run on the east and parallels Jones Falls to the south, Falls Road on the west, and Ruxton Road on the north.

Bosley's Adventure resulted from the consolidation of five smaller land grants by John Bosley in the years from 1743 to 1763. During these twenty years, in addition to his own grants, he acquired three other neighboring properties and part of a fourth: Betty's Adventure, originally granted to Edward Rusting in 1724 for a hundred acres; Miller's Choice, granted directly by Charles Calvert, Fifth Lord Baltimore, to John Gardner in 1722 for 250 acres; Cook's Purchase, granted to Thomas Cook in 1741 for fifty acres, and nineteen acres of the Hopyard originally granted in 1695 to Hector McClane. These properties were in addition to the two grants received by Bosley from the Proprietor's Land Office: Bosley's Meadow granted in 1743 for twenty-one acres and the Great Tobacco Maker's Loss, dating to 1762, for fifteen acres.[1]

These acreages totaled 454 but in 1764, when they were resurveyed at Bosley's request for a guarantee of ownership or patent, the area was found actually to contain 408 acres as well as ninety-one acres of surplus land (ungranted, vacant property that lay between or adjacent to granted portions) for a total of 499 acres. The deputy surveyor for Baltimore County, William Smith, described the vacant land as containing "about 200 panels of fence, 80 apple trees and about 40 acres cultivated very much worne." John Bosley thus had increased his holdings from his original grants of thirty-six acres to nearly 500 by the time he died in 1772. He was the largest single landholder in the neighborhood. At his death, Bosley bequeathed the resurveyed land to his son Walter.[2]

When Walter died shortly thereafter without heirs, the property passed to his surviving brother Joseph. Unfortunately, Joseph died in 1776 leaving a pregnant wife and nine children. His will provided that all real estate be equally divided among his five sons, Joshua, John, Daniel, William, Philip, and the unborn child (if a male) upon reaching their legal age. There was a curious small debt of three pounds to Captain Charles Ridgely of Hampton, but otherwise Joseph left a prosperous and sizable estate.[3] Not including Bosley's Adventure and other extensive land holdings, his goods and chattels alone were valued at 2,651 pounds. These included all types of farm equipment, livestock, and twenty slaves. He left over a ton of tobacco valued at only twenty-five pounds and currency of 454 pounds. Such seldom seen luxuries as a silver watch, silver buckles, and seven Bibles confirm that Mr. Bosley was very well-to-do for the period.[4]

Mary, Joseph's widow, soon married one Amos Ogden, described unflatteringly in a chancery record as "her overseer, a man of indifferent character." Because Mary had refused her devise and claimed her dower right to one-third of the estate, Amos Ogden assumed title to approximately 250 acres of Bosley's Adventure.[5] In 1779 they released their rights to the acreage, which her son Joshua occupied, for five pounds.[6]

As the only adult of Joseph's five male heirs, Joshua was made executor of his father's will and was charged with the responsibility of holding the lands until each brother reached the age of twenty-one, at which time he had full power to transfer to them their rightful shares. Accordingly, in 1782 Joshua deeded fifty acres of Bosley's Adventure to his younger brother John, as well as two other parcels outside of our study area.[7] In an apparently unrecorded deed, Philip received the portion of Bosley's Adventure to which he was entitled but sold these 204 acres back to Joshua in 1786 for "700 pounds specie."[8] Thus Joshua had acquired 454 acres of the original tract settled by his grandfather.

Joshua sold his portion of Bosley's Adventure in three separate transactions. In 1789 he sold 122 acres to Frederick Hook, a "shoemaker, from Baltimore town" for 213 pounds and sixty-seven acres to Michael Krener, also of the city. The third and largest parcel of 318 acres was conveyed to Francis Dawes and William Scott, both of Baltimore County, for the sum of 757 pounds.[9] It appears that the first John Bosley residence, indicated by the 1798 Federal Direct Tax Assessment, was located on the southwestern quarter of the property adjoining Jones Falls. This site was situated on the Miller's Choice portion of Bosley's Adventure purchased by Hook and serviced by Falls Road.[10]

In the first U.S. Census, published in 1790, Joshua's household, residing in Back-River–Upper Hundred, was listed as including seven free whites and ten slaves. His brother William's household was recorded in the same district with eight free whites and five slaves.

Though Joseph's sons Daniel and William did not receive any Bosley's Adventure property, they were assigned other land from their father's estate. William's son later purchased in 1817, from John's widow Ann, the fifty acres held by her and "several old huts fit for fuel."[11] He held the property only a year before selling it to Nicholas Ruxton Moore's widow in 1818, when this last remaining parcel of Bosley's Adventure passed from the family.[12]

Neither Dawes nor Scott lived on Bosley's Adventure but rather held the land for speculation. By February 1795, hero of the Revolution and future congressman Colonel Nicholas Ruxton Moore had purchased this 318 acres of Bosley's Adventure for 2,000 pounds.[13] Evidently Moore soon constructed his home, for the assessment of 1798 values the property at $1,884 and describes the structures as a framed dwelling house of one story, 16 by 32 feet, a stone milk house and stone meat house, both 12 by 12, and other outbuildings.

Nicholas Ruxton Moore

Nicholas Ruxton Moore was born on a two hundred-acre farm in Gunpowder Manor, Baltimore County, on September 29, 1756, to

James Moore Jr. and Hanna Wilmott Moore. His uncle, Nicholas Ruxton Gay, was a deputy surveyor for Baltimore County and worked in the area that now bears the Ruxton name. Gay was an early settler of Baltimore town and came to own much property in the city and Baltimore County. In 1776 Gay died a very old man and left his estate to his nephew, who as a result became a wealthy young man at the age of twenty.

Two years before he received the bequest, Moore had joined Captain Mordecai Gist's Independent Cadets, one of the first local units formed in anticipation of the Revolution. Moore was commissioned third lieutenant in March 1776 and was soon dispatched by the Council of Safety, Maryland's revolutionary governing council, to Annapolis where he took charge of the city's defenses. Because of Tory sentiment in the colonial capital and for fear such preparations in and of themselves might actually invite attack, Moore was reassigned late in 1776 as first lieutenant at the Fort McHenry preparations at Whetstone Point.

Moore received a Congressional commission as a lieutenant in 1777 with orders to raise a cavalry company. In the fall, he and his unit saw action at the battles at Brandywine and Germantown under the command of General Casimir Pulaski. After these campaigns, he resigned his commission to return to Maryland to raise a second mounted cavalry unit that became known as the Baltimore Light Dragoons.

In February 1781, Moore, now a captain, again saw active duty when ordered to the James River area of Virginia to provide cavalry support for Marquis de Lafayette. There were no major engagements with the British units under Generals Cornwallis or Tarleton – only raids against each others' territory – so Moore and his dragoons returned to Baltimore in late summer. On September 8, General George Washington, en route to the siege at Yorktown, arrived in Baltimore and was escorted to his headquarters at the Fountain Inn (at the northeast corner of today's Light and Redwood Streets). The dragoons were a select group of gentlemen chosen for their position in the community and were responsible for their own equipment and mounts. They also served an important ceremonial function for city visitors during this period.

After the Revolution, Moore became prominent in the civic and business affairs of Baltimore. Regrettably, his wife Elizabeth

Nicholas Ruxton Moore (1756-1816), Revolutionary hero, civic leader, congressman, and philanthropist for whom the community is named.
(Courtesy Society of the Cincinnati, Washington, D.C.)

Located on the north side of Circle Road, just west of Roland Run, this stone spring house served the Nicholas Ruxton Moore farm from 1784 to 1824.
(Collection of the author.)

died in 1784 and their children all died as infants. When the U. S. Constitution was ratified in 1788, Moore was one of two state marshals in charge of the elaborate festivities and celebrations. In 1792, Moore married Sarah Kelso, with whom he had one son and three daughters. In this post-Revolutionary time, Moore lived on his four hundred-acre farm in what is now the Brooklyn area of Baltimore city. In 1794, in anticipation of the December settlement on the Bosley's Adventure property, he sold the farm and the city townhouse that he had kept so he could be close to his business interests. Seeking to raise his new family in a healthier environment than the city had provided for his first family, he soon moved to his new 350-acre Baltimore County farm.

As he prepared to move, Moore and his company of cavalry were again ordered into service by Maryland's Governor Thomas Sim Lee during the Whisky Rebellion. The Secretary of War had ordered Lee to activate the Maryland Militia for service in quelling this challenge to Federal authority in Pennsylvania. Fortunately, the disturbance soon ended and Moore's move to the farm and a new home was completed.

In his politics Moore was a Republican and a Jeffersonian. After being an elector in the presidential election of 1800 and serving in the Maryland House of Delegates, Moore was elected to the U. S. Congress in 1803 and served until 1816. These were critical times for the young country and Moore was involved in many of the great debates of the day such as the Louisiana Purchase, the Embargo of 1807, and the Non-Intercourse Acts of 1809. The latter two acts threatened to embroil the country in the great European power struggle and were precursors to the War of 1812. With war preparations under way, Moore was appointed lieutenant colonel of the Sixth Regimental Cavalry District of Maryland under General Sam Smith. There is no record of his seeing battle during the events of September 1814 in the defense of Baltimore, but he was in the field with his units operating east and north of the city. After the war, Moore returned to the comfort of his home and his congressional seat, but was taken sick and died in 1816.[14]

Moore was typical of so many unsung heroes to whom we owe our independence. He and others like him were the driving force behind the American Revolution. They had everything to lose —

their wealth, positions, and, if caught, possibly their lives. After the British came the challenge of nation building, which, despite the turbulence, was equally successful.

Ruxton folklore speculates about where Moore was laid to rest. Newspaper accounts mention that he was buried on the farm, but none give a precise location. Since America was largely a rural society, it was customary in the early 1800's for each farm to have a family cemetery or to share a plot of land with neighbors for this purpose. The only reference located during this study of Bosley's Adventure that precisely designates a graveyard is in the 1855 deed by which Samuel Fishpaw granted portions of Hector's Hopyard to James McDaniel. As noted on the grant map, the properties share a common border: Bosley's Adventure's southern boundary is the Hopyard's northern line. In describing the north line of the Hopyard, the deed states:

> . . . running on a part of said line S 88 W 29 perches to the northeast corner of a parcel of land reserved as a graveyard the following three courses: S 20 E 6 perches, S 69 W 8 perches, N 20 W 9 perches and then to the aforesaid line.[15]

By a reasonably accurate interpretation of the above, the shared graveyard of the two farms sat on the property line, two hundred feet due west of the bridge that today carries Club Road over Roland Run. This is the probable grave site of Ruxton Moore. With the passage of time, the site fell into disrepair and met the unfortunate fate of other similar small family plots in the area.

In May 1819, widow Sarah Moore, as an executor of her late husband's will, petitioned the court for permission to sell the farm.[16] She argued that "the farm at present is unproductive, and that for want of skill and the means necessary to the management and the preservation of said Estate, the improvements thereupon must soon decay and be in a ruinous condition, and the land itself much lessened in value."

Court permission and bonding problems were worked out and Sarah Moore, as trustee for the sale, advertised the property in the August 8, 1821, issues of the *Baltimore American* and *Commercial Daily Advertiser*. She described it as a valuable farm located about 7 1/2 miles from Baltimore City on the Falls Turnpike Road and well known as the residence of the late Colonel Nicholas Ruxton Moore. According to the advertisement, which contrasts sharply with the earlier court deposition, Moore cut ninety tons of timothy and clover hay from it in one year. Continuing:

> This farm contains upwards of 350 acres of limestone land, 40 of which are in wood and at least 100 in meadow (principally natural). It abounds with springs mostly limestone; there is not a field of it which is not watered. There are also three orchards of choice fruit. A frame dwelling house, stone spring and meat houses; a large barn, quarter and overseer's house.[17]

The Hopkins atlas of 1877 shows the farm's property line and structural detail fifty-five years later, which helps to locate it today. The site of the former Moore home is what is now the second property after crossing the Roland Run bridge on the north side of Circle Road. The spring house referred to above is shown in the atlas in a cluster of three stone and three wooden frame buildings. Although the spring has been diverted, the stone spring house remains and is in sound structural condition having been well maintained by past and current owners.

This was a most unfortunate time to sell property. The Panic of 1819 had caused widespread bank failures and a five-year period of agricultural and industrial deflation. As a result, Sarah did not receive any public bids for the farm, but eventually was offered $6,500 through a private sale to William McConkey. The court agreed to the sale and the transfer was executed in 1824.[18]

William McConkey held the property for the next twenty years, until his death in 1844. His son George fell heir to this portion of Bosley's Adventure but in a series of conveyances beginning in 1845 sold off the property. The northwestern portion of the farm (167 acres) adjoining Falls Road was purchased by a group involved with the Rockland Mill Works, consisting of William Tagart and Thomas, John, and Robert Wright.[19] According to the Hopkins atlas and the relative cost of the properties, it appears that no improvements had been made on this part of the farm at the time of the sale. The historic maps show these individuals living adjacent to the village of Rockland on the western side of the property.

In 1855, Henry W. Hiser purchased the remaining 183 acres of

George and Elizabeth McConkey (circa 1850). William McConkey purchased the 350-acre Moore farm for $6,500. When he died in 1844 the property was inherited by his son George. *(Maryland Historical Society, Rider Collection.)*

Bosley's Adventure from George McConkey for $12,500.[20] This eastern half of Bosley's Adventure contained the residence and buildings described in the Nicholas Ruxton Moore sale notice. Renaming the farm "Belvale," Hiser added to the acreage which had been subdivided since the Moores' residency. In 1859, he purchased the forty-two acre tract of land lying between the railroad on the east and Roland Run. This part of Young Man's Adventure was obtained from Edward Rider Jr. at a cost of $8,500.[21] The land's attractiveness was agricultural, being fertile and well watered, as part of it remains today, having recently been reclaimed from residential use for the Roland Run/Lake Roland watershed.

Sarah Hiser, Henry's widow, sold the farm, now consisting of 225 acres, to William A. and Charles D. Fisher in August 1886.[22] The following year, the property was divided into numerous home sites ranging in size from one-and-a-half to twelve acres. Charles's estate, according to the Hopkins and Bromley maps (*see front and back endsheets*), was known as Rolandvue and still stands near the summit of the road bearing this name, part of the Samuel's Hope property.

In February 1887, the *Baltimore Sun* carried an announcement of "preparations to build a village near Lake Roland" and referred to "Ruxton" for the first time.

> An avenue thirty feet wide will be finished from the property known as Ruxton to the Charles Street Avenue [Boyce Ave.] about a mile distant as soon as spring opens, it having been about half completed. Another avenue, an extension of the one under way, will be carried to the Falls Road.[23]

The unyielding pressure of urbanization from the growth of an industrial Baltimore led to further land subdivision and development. What happened to Bosley's Adventure is typical of the fate of other properties in the Roland Run Valley. The character of this community changed radically during the late 1800s and early 1900s from a rural one of gentleman farmers to that of a suburban neighborhood serving as a haven from the summer heat and congestion of the city. The railroad, still the primary link with Baltimore, lost some of its wheat, grain, and livestock cargo to passenger business at familiar stops that came to be known by residents as Lake Station, Sherwood, Rider's Switch, and Ruxton.

·4·

Young Man's Adventure

---◦◦◦---

To the east of Roland Run and Bosley's Adventure lies Young Man's Adventure, a square two hundred-acre parcel, which also derives its origin from the 1694 warrant to Thomas Hooker.[1] The Ruxton commercial area now occupies the center of this grant which described the property in part as

> . . . lying in Baltimore County above the field of the Patapsco River upon Jones Falls near unto a ridge called by the name of Britain, Beginning at a bounded white oak standing on the east side of a run, being the eastern of most branch of Jones Falls, standing in a line of a parcel of land of Hector McClane's and running North 185 perches up the run, then East 185 perches, then South 185 perches, then with a direct line to the first bounded tree containing, and hence laid out two hundred acres.

The land first passed to Thomas Sparrow (as in Sparrows Point) and then in 1704 to his son-in-law William Coale of Anne Arundel County.[2] In 1710, Coale purchased additional properties to the immediate north known as Martinton and Martin's Addition, each containing one hundred acres. William died in 1715 and Young Man's Adventure was inherited by his son Thomas, while the Martinton and Martin's Addition lands were bequeathed to his son Samuel.[3] Apparently, Samuel died without heirs and these lands later passed to Thomas, as provided for in their father's will.

In 1741, Thomas sold Young Man's Adventure, Martinton and Martin's Addition to his older brother William for "100 pounds Sterling of Great Britain."[4] In 1743, William received a grant of twenty-seven acres of vacant land known as Coale's Good Luck, lying between Martin's Addition and Young Man's Adventure.[5] William died at West River in Anne Arundel County in 1761 and never lived on these properties. Prior to William's death, however, both of his sons, Samuel and William Jr., had taken up residence on the land during the early 1740s or possibly earlier: Samuel, on the Martinton, Martin's Addition, and Good Luck properties and William Jr. on Young Man's Adventure. Actual ownership of these grants passed to William Jr. and Samuel upon their father's death.[6] In 1756, William Jr. was granted an additional thirty-nine acres called Coale's Discovery.[7] This rectangular piece of vacant land adjoined the entire eastern line of Young Man's Adventure. In 1760 William Sr. and Jr. were recorded as contributing to Quaker relief for the sufferers of a fire in Boston.

In 1769, William Jr. appears as a resident of the county in the petitions for and against removal of the county seat from Joppa to Baltimore. The assessment of 1783 also lists William Jr. as head of a household in Back River-Upper Hundred as this portion of the county was then called. The Census of 1790 shows William Jr. as head of a household with two free white males over sixteen, two under sixteen, six free females, and seven slaves.

For over fifty years William Jr. lived on Young Man's Adventure, raising two sons (both married Bowens of Samuel's Hope) and three daughters. The Federal Assessment of 1798 describes details of the 230-acre Britain Ridge farm with two frame dwelling houses, 25 by 28 feet and 16 by 20 feet, a barn 24 by 40 feet, and a stable 12 by 24 feet, all valued at $1,380. When he died a widower in 1809 at eighty-seven years of age, his oldest son, William Harvey Coale, was bequeathed Young Man's Adventure. He left the United States, however, to live in England and forfeited the farm to his younger brother, Philemon.[8] Because of his brother's absence and his father's advanced age, Philemon occupied and ran the farm for some time prior to acquiring title to the property.

William's Coale's inventory, witnessed by neighbors Solomon Bowen and Joseph Wheeler, revealed a prosperous, well developed, and nearly self-sufficient farming operation valued at $2,648.60. The chattels and farm inventory showed the variety of undertakings that were required of the typical Maryland farmer in the still largely agricultural society of the early nineteenth century. Also revealed is the

The Coale springhouse (ca. 1828) as it looked in 1900. Typical of early nineteenth-century outbuildings that provided cooling for food preservation and water, this restored structure is located in the center of Young Man's Adventure at what is now 1317 Boyce Avenue in Ruxton. *(Collection of the author.)*

continuing importance of slavery in supporting this way of life. In fact, Coale's most valuable possessions were five slaves with Peter, the youngest at nineteen years of age, valued at $350.

Other items of interest from this 1809 inventory were a wide assortment of livestock including pigs, sheep, cows, bulls, and horses; also, farm produce, a loft of corn (125 bushels at $4.00 per), 130 bushels of rye at $1 per, sixty bushels of oats, forty bushels of rye in the ground, 130 bushels of potatoes, three tons of hay, twenty-seven bushels of beans, 1,722 pounds of pork at 5 cents per pound, and many types of farm, carpenter, and cooper tools and equipment.[9]

Because of the inaccuracies of early surveying and the potential for disputes, Philemon had Young Man's Adventure resurveyed in 1816 for the purpose of securing a guarantee of ownership from the state. The new survey showed the property to contain 244 1/2 acres, which included the thirty-nine-acre Coale's Discovery parcel. Also added were thirteen acres of bordering vacant land that had not been previously granted or included in the original grant of 1694. This property contained "342 panels of middling good fence and four old apple trees," all valued at $15.68.[10]

Philemon Coale lived on and worked the farm until he died in 1838 at the age of sixty-six.[11] He married twice, raised fifteen children, rallied to the defense of Baltimore in September of 1814 as a member of the Maryland Militia under the command of Colonel Nicholas Ruxton Moore, and was a trustee and founder of both the Hunt's Methodist Church and the neighborhood school on Joppa Road. He also contested, along with his neighbors, the encroachment of the railroad that cut a sixty-six-foot wide strip through their farms.[12] Philemon Coale's springhouse, built in 1828, still stands proudly, if somewhat worn, off the south side of Boyce Avenue opposite the Church of the Good Shepherd.

Philemon's will ordered that the farm and personal property were to be sold during the year 1845 at public auction. Accordingly, in November of that year, the following appeared in the *Baltimore Sun* with a long list of farm equipment, livestock, and personal items.

> FOR SALE – 243 acres, 50 in wood the rest cleared and in good state of cultivation . . . improvements – frame dwelling, old barn and other necessary out houses . . . situated in a good neighborhood with limestone in abundance in immediate vicinity thereof which offers great facility to the improvement of the same.[13]

Not until 1847 was the farm finally sold to Edward Rider Sr., the highest bidder, for $6,005.[14] Rider was a respected and well known resident of the area having purchased a farm from William Ridgely to the north known as Thornton in 1827. When Edward Rider's son, Edward Jr., married Rebecca McConkey in 1856, Young Man's Adventure was sold to him for $10,000 and renamed Malvern.[15] In the same year, Edward Jr. began construction of a large three-story frame residence that adjoined the stone cottage built by Philemon Coale in 1806. The new home housed his wife and children for the next fifty years.

With a western exposure toward the railroad, the home was located at the end of a drive (now Locust Avenue) from Bellona

Malvern, Edward Rider Jr's residence. Edward Rider Sr. purchased Young Man's Adventure in 1845 and sold the property to his son ten years later. Edward Jr. then built this large three-story frame home with access from Bellona Avenue. The residence, destroyed by fire in 1910, was located at 1402 Locust Avenue, at the crest of the hill. *(Maryland Historical Society, Rider Collection.)*

Avenue. Edward Rider Jr. was a successful farmer but he had other activities in the brokerage and banking businesses and an interest in the Northern Central Railroad. He sold forty-two acres of the farm to Henry Hiser, his neighbor to the west (Bosley's Adventure) in 1859.[16] This area included the western portion of Young Man's Adventure lying between Roland Run and the railroad. That which remained was later described, richly embellished, as

> One of the beautiful estates of the Ninth District. On every side stretch tilled fields and meadows that lie velvety and green beneath

Mary Rider Haslup residence. The first child of Edward and Rebecca Rider, Mary was born in 1856. In 1877, she married John Haslup, a Methodist circuit rider who died ten years later. She was president of the Women's Christian Temperance Union of Maryland for forty-two years. Her residence, one of the first homes built when Malvern was subdivided in the early 1890s, still stands on the northeast corner of Malvern Avenue and Ruxton Road. *(Maryland Historical Society, Rider Collection.)*

Above, left: Edward Rider Jr., his wife Rebecca, and three of their seven children in 1860. At right is Mary Rider (Haslup), the eldest child, who later in life recalled trains passing through the farm loaded with Union soldiers and Lincoln's funeral train. *(Maryland Historical Society, Rider Collection.)*

Left: Rebecca Rider (Mrs. Edward Rider Jr.) and four of her grown children on the front porch at Malvern ca. 1900. Left to right, Eliza, Rebecca, Edward H., Florence, and Dr. William B. *(Maryland Historical Society, Rider Collection.)*

the summer sun. The 240 acres comprising the farm have been placed beneath excellent cultivation and made to produce bountiful harvests of the various cereals to which the soil is adapted. This is the home of the Rider family a fitting abode for people of wealth and culture.[17]

The 1857 Robert Taylor map of the City and County of Baltimore identifies Young Man's Adventure and Powder Mill Road (Bellona Avenue). Ruxton was still an agricultural area and urban pressures for subdivision had not yet begun. However, by 1877, the Hopkins atlas shows the Edward Rider estate of Malvern and other neighborhood properties in revealing detail. This atlas has been an invaluable resource in preparing this survey. It shows individual property lines, private driveways, streams, placement and construction of structures, etc. Interestingly, many of the Ruxton property lines of 1877 still conformed to the original grant boundaries laid out in 1694.

The continuing pressures of urbanization affected the Malvern property as well as others in the Roland Run Valley, however, and led Rider in 1894 (three years before his death) to sell portions of the farm for a development. Roland Park, an experiment in early suburban development, had only just been established; this new planned development, called Ruxton Heights, was similarly ambitious. Generous terms were offered on a plat of the development as encouragement to prospective buyers to "Think Fast, Act Quick." The advertisement continued: "Baltimore's most beautiful suburb . . . Clean, healthy, picturesque, natural drainage, thoroughly accessible . . . lots from $200-$500 . . . small payments, no interest, no taxes, no mortgages."[18]

Further pressure for subdivision resulted in 1910 when the sparks from an open fireplace burned the Rider and Coale home to the ground. The *Baltimore Sun* for December 30 summed up the loss:

> The mansion had a commanding view of the surrounding country, as it stood on Ruxton Hill and was at one time in the center of a large tract of land that took in a greater portion of that part of the county and when news of its destruction spread many instances that had happened about it were recalled.

·5·

Martinton and
Martin's Addition

To the north of Young Man's Adventure lie the tracts of Martinton and Martin's Addition, granted in two parcels of a hundred acres each to John Martin of Baltimore County in 1703 and 1704.[1]

Much of this land today includes areas of the Riderwood and Sherwood communities. Martin, or a tenant, appears to have taken residence on the property soon after the grants were made. When the land was sold to William Coale of Anne Arundel County in 1710 for "35 pounds good and lawful money of England," the deed described the farm as having a dwelling house, tenant houses, yards, barns, stables, tobacco houses, gardens, and orchards.[2]

As related in the preceding section on Young Man's Adventure, there is no evidence that Coale ever lived on Martinton or Martin's Addition, or on Young Man's Adventure to the south, which he also owned. At the time, he had large holdings in the West River area of Anne Arundel county and died there in 1715. In his will, his son Samuel received Martinton and Martin's Addition while son Thomas was bequeathed the neighboring Young Man's Adventure. Thomas was also to receive Martinton and Martin's Addition proportion if Samuel died without heirs.[3] As previously mentioned, this evidently happened as Thomas sold all three properties in 1741 to his older brother William for 100 pounds.[4] In 1743, William acquired a twenty-seven-acre grant for Coale's Good Luck, a piece of vacant land situated between Martin's Addition and Young Man's Adventure.[5]

William sold ten acres of Martinton for ten pounds in 1743 to Nicholas Haile, a "planter of Baltimore County," who shortly afterward established a mill on the site to answer the needs of this growing agricultural area.[6] Haile operated this enterprise on the northwest side of Roland Run at what is now Joppa and Thornton Roads, until 1780 when it was sold to Charles Ridgely of William for fifty pounds.[7] Ridgely operated the mill for thirty years until his death.

Charles Ridgely of William hardly fits our description of a "middling planter." A gentleman of prominence and wealth, Charles of William was first cousin to Charles Ridgely of Hampton and was well known to his contemporaries as "Blackheaded Charles Ridgely." A successful merchant, planter, and public personality in his own right, he held various local and state public offices that included the Committee of Observation, judgeships in the county and orphans' court, the State Constitutional Convention (where he represented Baltimore County), the Maryland House of Delegates, and the State Senate.[8]

The 1790 Census of Back-River Upper Hundred identifies the former Haile mill site simply as "Charles Ridgely (of Wm.'s Quarter) – 8 slaves." He did not live there but owned and operated the mill commercially. The 1798 Assessment shows that Charles owned 150 acres of the Selsed property which adjoined Martinton to the north, with an "old frame dwelling house 16 x 20 feet, a stable and barn." Eight slaves are again noted. Selsed was a nine hundred-acre grant to Rowland Thornburg in 1694 that now includes portions of the Village Green and the Seminary Avenue and Thornton Road residential areas. Mr. Thornburg's given name is the probable source of the name of the stream that passes through the property.

In 1810, Ridgely died at his home plantation on the Patapsco River, one of the few residences noted on the Griffith map of 1794.[9] He left six plantations in Baltimore and Anne Arundel Counties, 2,000 acres of land in all, with sixty-four slaves. The mill passed to his son William Augustus Ridgely.[10] The structure itself remained for many years, even if somewhat ill-focused as to its purpose, being referred to as a "woolen mill," a "cotton factory," and "old grist mill" on the Sidney, Chiffelle and Taylor maps.

As noted previously, upon William Coale's death in 1761, Young Man's Adventure was bequeathed to his son William Jr. Martinton,

Edward Gorsuch Rider Sr. and his wife Rachael purchased 167 acres of Martinton from William Augustus Ridgely in 1824. This property, in what is now Riderwood, and other adjacent lands purchased by Edward Rider Sr. were named Thornton. *(Maryland Historical Society, Rider Collection.)*

Martin's Addition, and Coale's Good Luck were given to son Samuel. It appears that both had taken residence on these properties sometime before, but the tracts did not formally pass to them until their father's death.

In 1790, Samuel sold for twenty pounds all that part of Martinton that "lies on the north side of the Court Road" (Joppa Road) to his son Philip, as well as the right to take wood "for the repair of said plantation with fence rails and firewood" from Martin's Addition.[11] The 1798 Federal Assessment shows Samuel with 140 acres of the property and thirty-two acres of Coale's Good Luck with an old frame dwelling house 15 by 25 feet, a barn 24 by 30 feet, a stone stable 12 by 32 feet, and other outbuildings.

In his will dated 1807, Samuel divided the remaining parts of his property among his children without mentioning either of the two tracts by name. Son William received the land on the west side of Roland Run in addition to Coale's Good Luck, now renamed Coale's Harbor in a resurvey (1764).[12] The Hopkins map *(see front endsheet)* shows a "Samuel Cole," William's son, still in possession of the tract in 1877. Son John received all the remaining land that consisted most-ly of the Martin's Addition acreage and the area of Martinton lying between Roland Run and the western line of Martin's Addition.

Several years after John Coale's death in 1817, his widow, Susan, married Lewis Roberts. They remained on the property, then known as Walnut Hill, and are shown on all referenced maps. Susan also received from her husband Reisterstown Turnpike and Union Bank of Maryland stock. Roberts passed the farm to his son Lewis J., who subdivided the property in 1886.[13]

An additional fifty acres of the Martinton property, including portions of the Roland Run stream held by William and Philip Coale on the northern side of Joppa Road, were purchased by William Augustus Ridgely in 1812 and 1813.[14] This property was adjacent to and complemented the mill site that he had earlier acquired from his father. Ten years later he sold all these properties to the gentleman whose name the area now carries, Edward Rider Sr. Ridgely's land in the area also included part of Gotts Hope (bordering Martin's Addition to the northeast) for a total purchase by Rider of 167 acres at a cost of $9,221.[15] Over the years, Rider acquired more of the Selsed property to the north and Ford's Choice. He died in 1866 after a distinguished and successful career centering on his farm, grain mill, and lime burning business. His property was divided among his children as shown on the Hopkins map of 1877 *(see front endsheet)*.

Located off the northwest corner of Martin's Addition was a small parcel called "Good Luck," eight and one-half acres granted to a Samuel Livingston, a teacher, in 1777.[16] Shortly thereafter, he established a residence and separate neighborhood schoolhouse referred to as the Livingston Academy. In 1827, after Livingston's death, the property was acquired by Richard Gott (Gott's Hope and Gott's Addition) and a half-acre lot containing the schoolhouse was sold off to a Nathan Ware. "On the Court Road leading from Hunt's Meeting to Towsontown," the property was now referred to as Ware's Schoolhouse. The deed described this land, in part, as "at the foot of a rough black oak on the edge of an old quarry on the south side of Sutter's Hill." Reserved for schoolhouse use was "a certain spring of water or fountain 27 perches off the road on Richard Gott's premises."[17]

In 1831 the plot changed hands again, this time to Julian Barron with the structure now described as "the stone academy thereon."[18] Two years later a more permanent arrangement was instituted "for the benefit of the neighborhood." A group of trustees was formed and ownership passed to them for $260.[19] The school is identified in the maps of the period and apparently remained intact well into the twentieth century when it was replaced by a small contemporary cottage that now occupies the site.

·6·

Hooker's Prosperity

In 1703, Benjamin Hooker of Baltimore County received a grant known as Hooker's Prosperity from a 1,000-acre warrant held by Dutton Lane, also of Baltimore County. This perfectly square parcel, 135 by 135 perches, was located off the east line of Young Man's Adventure and the north line of Samuel's Hope. Containing 114 acres, the property was assigned to William Wheeler in 1706.[1] Today this area contains all of East, South, and West Wind Roads and the eastern half of Malvern Avenue.

Shortly after receiving title, Wheeler and his wife Martha established and operated a tobacco and cattle plantation until his death in 1738.[2] His estate was valued at ninety-nine pounds, considerably less than the farms of his immediate neighbors. Among many items, Wheeler's most valuable possessions were sixteen head of cattle appraised at twenty-six pounds and thirty head of hogs at eight pounds, while 2,160 pounds of tobacco were valued at only five pounds sterling.[3]

Wheeler's estate suffered the effects of Maryland's tobacco market depression during this period so a five-pound evaluation was probably generous. The state's crop was evaluated as "second rate with English merchants refusing to buy," which caused a serious economic crisis as the commodity was still used as a common means of exchange and credit. The Tobacco Inspection Act of 1747 set standards and a quality control system that helped to restore the market.[4]

William Wheeler's property passed to his son Solomon, who further developed the farm into a successful and profitable operation that included two male slaves.[5] Solomon was listed in the

The funeral of the Methodist minister
Robert Strawbridge at the home of Joseph
Wheeler in Hooker's Prosperity in 1781.
*(Engraving by A. Hoen, Baltimore; collection
of the author.)*

T.C.Buckle.   The House where Rev. R. Strawbridge died, a

Lith. by A. Hoen & Co. Baltᵒ.

from the yard, of which his Funeral took place

Assessment of 1783 for a hundred acres in Back River-Upper Hundred. When he died in 1787, his estate was valued at 524 pounds.[6] The younger Wheeler had done so well that at his death four neighbors were listed as having outstanding debts to him, including Jacob Young of Hector's Hopyard for five pounds and Solomon Bowen of Samuel's Hope for four pounds. The farm was equally divided between Solomon Wheeler's sons, Joseph and Thomas. The former had already established a home on Hooker's Prosperity prior to his father's death.

Religion played an important part in the lives of the early planters in Baltimore County and the Wheelers were no exception. Methodism, founded in 1739 by John Wesley, an Anglican minister, used many lay preachers to spread the beliefs of the movement. Methodism began its strong influence in America when Wesley sent Robert Strawbridge to Maryland in 1766 to establish its first society at Sam's Creek in Frederick County. Working as a circuit preacher, Strawbridge soon pushed into Baltimore County and founded the first Methodist meeting place at the home of Daniel Evans (as in Evans Chapel Road), which is now the site of the Roland Park Country School. All three of the maps in this book from the 1850s show the site of the Evans Meeting House.

This popular movement had a significant local impact on the day-to-day religious life of this agricultural community. In Ruxton, lay preachers conducted services at the Wheeler home as well as at Phineas Hunt's (Beale's Discovery) for several years prior to construction of the first Hunt Meeting House, a log cabin, on Joppa Road in 1780. It was a major event for the neighborhood when Mr. Strawbridge came to preach. While speaking at the Hunt's Chapel in 1781, he was hosted at Joseph Wheeler's home, but unfortunately, took sick and died. According to the Hunt Church's history:

> The house was not large enough to accommodate the vast concourse of persons who desired to attend the funeral of him who had been their pastor in the wilderness. . . . The sermon was preached in the open air under the spreading branches of a walnut tree.[7]

Strawbridge was buried in the Wheeler family graveyard in the orchard a hundred yards south of the residence. This property today is located north of Malvern Avenue on the hillside at 308 North Wind Road. The walnut tree and grave became a symbol of religious

Engraving by A. Hoen of the Robert Strawbridge grave site. Loyal Methodists made pilgrimages to this site for many years until Strawbridge's remains were reinterred at Mt. Olivet Cemetery in Baltimore City in the 1860s. *(Maryland Historical Society.)*

remembrance. For a number of years after Strawbridge's death visits were made to the site by members of the local Methodist community. Strawbridge's remains were removed to the Bishop's Lot in Mount Olivet Cemetery in the 1860s.[7] As time went by and urbanization encroached still further, the walnut tree finally succumbed to age in 1914.

> The old Strawbridge walnut tree, which has been dear by reason of its association to Methodists throughout the country, has been cut down and the stump removed by workmen engaged in the grading of the ground around the new home of Mr. Samuel W. Lipincott, which is located close by the spot where the tree stood. It had been dying for a number of years and was mutilated by persons who had cut out pieces of the trunk for souvenirs.[8]

The Census of 1790 shows Joseph (but no mention of Thomas who apparently had moved away from the property yet still held title) as head of a seven-person household, owning seven slaves and living in Back River-Upper Hundred. The Federal Direct Assessment of 1798 records only Joseph Wheeler's half interest of 66 $1/2$ acres with a dwelling house 18 by 24 feet, valued at $50, a kitchen 16 by 16 feet, a hen house 10 by 10 feet, a log barn, and an old stable. Later the same year and after eleven years of joint ownership, although he never lived on the property, Thomas sold his half interest to his brother for 198 pounds.[9]

Joseph Wheeler and his wife, Sarah Smith from Beale's Discovery, whom he married in 1786, lived on Hooker's Prosperity for forty-one years after his father's death.[10] When Joseph died in 1828 the property was left to Sarah for the duration of her life.[11] He also bequeathed to each of his five children "one feather bed and milk cow." The farm was to be sold at auction after Sarah's death and the proceeds distributed equally to the children. His son Elijah continued to operate and live on the farm as is recorded in the assessment of 1833.

Joseph's daughter, Sarah Blackburn Wheeler, was still living on the property when it was sold by Elijah, acting as his father's executor, in 1847 for $1,725 to Daniel Lee of Baltimore County.[12] Identified on both the Sidney and Chiffelle maps and active in county real estate, Lee resided on the property. Excluded from the sale were two acres reserved for Sarah, which contained the family residence and the graveyard site. However, the following year this was also sold to Lee for $2,000. Neither of the deeds transferring Hooker's Prosperity to Daniel Lee in 1847 was actually recorded until 1872 when Lee prepared to sell the property to James Boyce of "Chestnut Summit," an estate that fronted Joppa Road. Boyce, a prominent local coal merchant and trader, paid $23,500 for the 134-acre parcel shown on the Hopkins map of 1877 *(see front endsheet)*. The Boyce estate contained this land that earlier had been known as Hooker's Prosperity and portions of a property to the north known as Gott's Hope, which ran all the way to what is now Towson. Lee reserved for the future his family's right to visit and maintain the graveyard.[13] After Boyce's death the property was subdivided into numerous four- to eight-acre lots as shown in the Bromley map of 1898 *(back endsheet)*.

· 7 ·

Beale's Discovery

The tract forming the northwestern portion of Ruxton was known as Beale's Discovery. This rectangular parcel of three hundred acres covered approximately the area west of Roland Run, north of Ruxton Road, and east of the Jones Falls Expressway and included land north of the Old Court and Joppa Roads intersection.

More recorded research has been done on Beale's Discovery than any other parcel in Ruxton primarily because of Hunt's Church and its proximity to the Green Spring Valley.[1] In the 1770s, Methodism was becoming a dominant force in the religious life of rural America, an influence reflected in the daily activities of the Hunt family, the church they founded, and the experiences that this provided the Back River-Upper Hundred neighborhood of Baltimore County.

Beale's Discovery was first granted to Thomas Crossing of Great Britain in 1703.[2] His brother and heir sold the property in the "fifth year of our Sovereign King George III" (1732), to John Smith of Calvert County for forty-five pounds. The deed stipulated that "all houses, edifices, buildings, lands, meadows, and savannahs" were included in the sale. Evidently settlement by a tenant farmer or squatter had taken place prior to the sale because both Crossing brothers remained in Britain.[3]

In 1743, John Smith of Calvert County, by then a captain and also recorded as "merchant," participated in an exchange of tracts with Walter Smith Jr. of the Freshes of Patuxent, Calvert County.[4] Walter Smith received Beale's Discovery of three hundred acres and

63

two large neighboring tracts known as Poor Jamaica Man's Plague (434 acres) and the Groves (700 acres) from Captain Smith in return for Walter's lands in Calvert County. He died the same year and the properties passed to his son, Walter Smith III.[5] Our focus is on the Beale's Discovery property; the others, notwithstanding that some are contiguous, lie outside this study of Ruxton.

Smith Jr.'s widow, Elizabeth (Chew) married Job Hunt shortly after her husband's death and had five sons by him before his death in 1753. In 1765, Walter III leased five hundred acres, "in consideration of natural love," to his mother.[6] The lease covered primarily the Beale's Discovery property. Elizabeth and four of her sons by Hunt (Job, Phineas, Samuel, and Henry) moved to the site shortly thereafter.

In the same period Smith also issued a series of long-term leases on other portions of the properties left to him by his father. One such forty-year, sixty-acre lease was given to William Odell in 1765 in return for his constructing a dwelling house and a separate kitchen, each to be 20 by 16 feet, and planting an orchard of two hundred trees.[7] This conceivably was done in anticipation of Elizabeth and her children moving to the Beale's Discovery property. In 1766, Smith sold off 102 acres of Poor Jamaica Man's Plague and Beale's Discovery to Dr. Thomas Johnson of Turkey Cock Hall, a neighbor to the west. This land stayed in the Johnson family for over two hundred years.[8]

In 1770, Walter Smith III established a deed of trust that included the Groves (700 acres), Poor Jamaica Man's Plague (434 acres), and Beale's Discovery (200 acres) with a certain John Hopkins.[9] In the agreement, Smith specified that after his death the properties were to be passed to his "half blood" brothers, Job, Samuel, and Phineas Hunt as tenants in common, with brother Henry receiving a specific two hundred acres of the Groves. When his will was probated two years later, these assigns came to pass.[10]

Elizabeth (Smith) Hunt served as executrix of the will of her son, Walter Smith III, and the following year (1773) married for a third time. In anticipation of her marriage to John Bond, an agreement was filed in which she gave up her rights of dower to her two sons, Samuel and Phineas, in the three tracts of Selsed, Poor Jamaica Man's Plague, and Beale's Discovery. This included all rights to "outhouses, gardens, buildings and improvements." Also guaranteed were the property rights of her sons against any potential future claim from Bond. In return, each son guaranteed their mother an annual annuity of thirty pounds for the rest of her life.[11]

The Assessment of 1783 shows the three brothers, Samuel, Phineas, and Job, owning property in Back River-Upper Hundred with Phineas in possession of 115 acres of the Beale's Discovery land. All three brothers were members of St. Thomas's Church despite their dedication to the new Methodist doctrine. As early as 1773, as we saw in the preceding section on Hooker's Prosperity, Phineas Hunt's home on Beale's Discovery was serving as the meeting house for the growing Methodist community. A log structure was constructed in 1780 on Phineas's land (the site of the present-day church) and in 1786 a 3/4-acre site was formally transferred by deed "for 20 shillings" to the trustees of Hunt's Methodist Episcopal Church, including, among others, John and Joshua Bowen, William Stone, and Samuel Hunt.[12]

The Federal Census of 1790 lists the separate households of Job, Samuel, and Phineas as well as John Bond Sr. and Jr. Despite strong religious convictions against the practice by the early Methodists, forty-one slaves were held among these households.

The Assessment of 1798 described in greater detail the Phineas Hunt property, now listed as 140 acres, that included portions of Beale's Discovery and part of Poor Jamaica Man's Plague. Phineas had two log dwelling houses (perhaps the same two that were noted in the 1764 deed to his mother), one log barn, and one old frame barn 30 by 50 feet. Job Hunt was shown to own portions of Smith's Plains and Beale's Discovery totaling 180 acres plus other lands and numerous buildings.

In 1809, Job Hunt died at the age of sixty-three and declared by his will that his properties were to be sold and the proceeds distributed among his six children; Job Jr., Johns, Sarah, Lewis, Elizabeth, Jesse and Miriam. This was to be done within six months of his youngest son, Jesse, reaching legal age. Job provided for freedom for all twelve of his slaves over various periods of time with one qualification: "Phillip shall go free in 11 years if he behaves himself."[13]

The Assessment of 1813 shows "Doc" Thomas Johnson of neighboring Turkey Cock Hall with a hundred acres of Beale's Discovery and Phineas Hunt with 190.

In 1813, for $2,500, Johns Hunt purchased from his brother, Job Jr., a coppersmith of Frederick County, the rights to that portion of his father's land as yet unsold.[14] In March of the following year all six children petitioned the Court of Baltimore County to appoint a trustee to sell the properties as directed in the will. Johns was the high bidder for 502 acres at $48.50 per acre. This resulted in $6,086 being distributed to each of his brothers and sisters with the exception of Job Hunt who, unfortunately for him, had sold his interest for considerably less the year before.[15]

Johns Hunt died at the age of 59 in 1826. He was buried in the Hunt's graveyard, the only surviving family cemetery in Ruxton, with the following tribute on his stone.

> Sincere in devotion, faithful in friendship, kind and affectionate to those dependent on him. He rests in humble hope of a joyful resurrection. Tis great to pass and think in what a brighter world than this his spirit shines. How very near he is to Jesus.

A confirming deed was issued the same year as Johns Hunt's death after a second church, more suitable for the growing society, was constructed. Trustees listed at that time were Samuel C. Hunt, John Kelso, Philemon Coale, Thomas Watts, and Wesley Coale.[16]

At the age of eighty-five, Phineas Hunt died on February 6, 1837. He is buried in the surviving Hunt family burying ground several hundred yards west of the church between Joppa and Old Court Roads. "The attendance at his funeral was numerous and respectful for no one could help loving the old man." Phineas had no children and left his plantation "where on I now reside" to his nephew Jesse Hunt, who earlier had the honor of serving as mayor of Baltimore from 1832-1835.[17]

Phineas was later described by Rebecca Rider, daughter of Edward Rider of Thornton, who had known him from her early childhood. "He wore knee britches, his hair was curly and he allowed it to grow long and fall over his shoulders. . . . a man noted for his piety, usefulness and liberality."[18]

Many of the early families of Ruxton were associated with Hunt's Church and the Methodist movement. In the records of the church there is recurring mention of the area's early planters and residents. The meeting house, in addition to its religious value, served as a center for the neighborhood's cultural and social life.[19]

The Hunt family graveyard and the headstone of Johns Hunt are adjacent to Phineas Hunt's home and west of Hunt's Church. This is the only family cemetery still existing in the Ruxton area. *(Collection of the author.)*

·8·

The Baltimore & Susquehanna Railroad

---◄═•═►---

A major catalyst for change in the Roland Run Valley has been the railroad that has bisected the area since 1832. In August 1827, the Baltimore & Susquehanna Railroad was incorporated by an act of the Maryland legislature. Thus began local efforts to secure for Baltimore the trade of the Susquehanna River Valley.[1] Soon a corps of engineers was charting and surveying the most practical route between Baltimore and Wrightsville on the Susquehanna via York. Their efforts took them through the middle of what is now Ruxton.

As it was necessary for the railroad to acquire rights-of-way where tracks were to be laid, a sixty-six-foot path was soon planned through six of the local properties. All affected property owners turned down initial offers from the railroad and an out-of-court settlement could not be reached. It was then ordered that an impartial jury of twenty county inhabitants not related to either party (resident or railroad) be selected to determine the extent of the potential damages.

The jury first met on Solomon Bowen's property on February 14, 1832, to be shown the location of the proposed route of the road. From there they went to the farms of the others. The result of this process was unfortunate for the residents, as the jury found no damages inflicted on them and consequently awarded no compensation. In the opinion of the jury, none of the affected property owners was harmed by the railroad. Evidently it was felt that the road would enhance property values by providing easy access to city markets for

This 1838 bank note is typical of instruments that financed the construction of the Baltimore & Susquehanna Railroad. It depicts an English locomotive of the type used on the railroad in the late 1830s. The railroad's financial difficulties were chronic, but its economic and cultural impact was immense. *(Collection of the author.)*

produce and livestock. Travel time to Baltimore City would be cut from three hours to less than one.

To the farmers, however, the road seemed an intrusion that served little purpose other than to disturb the peaceful tranquility of the Valley, frighten the livestock, and act as a fire hazard. Rather than being a business asset as the railroad claimed, the road made farmers further out in the country more competitive. Nevertheless, by the process of condemnation property was taken from the farms of Solomon Bowen (3 3/4 acres), Philemon Coale (4 3/4 acres), Samuel Coale (3/4-acre), Lewis Roberts (2 acres), and Elijah Fishpaw (1/8-acre). For the Westminster branch that followed the Jones Falls to the west, property (4 acres) was condemned from Richard Hook's portion of Bosley's Adventure and (7 1/4 acres) from the Bellona Gunpowder Company.[2]

By 1838, sixty miles of the railroad had been completed to York, Pennsylvania. The rail trip to York took four hours at a cost of $1.75.

Despite recurring financial problems, passenger and freight tonnage continued to grow through the rest of the nineteenth century. Changing its name to the Northern Central in 1855, the railroad became a major supply and troop transport carrier during the Civil War. Its link with the North via Baltimore and Washington was cut several times by the destruction of several key bridges in Baltimore County. Local citizens, under orders from city and state civil authorities, sought to keep Union troops from passing through the Baltimore City for fear of igniting Baltimore's southern agitators. More violence was anticipated like that experienced on April 19, 1861, when the Sixth Massachusetts Regiment fought with a city mob while on its way to defend Washington.[3]

Two railroading incidents that occurred in Ruxton are of special interest. On the evening of July 4, 1856, a most tragic and ghastly event occurred several hundred yards north of the present-day Joppa Road bridge when two trains of the Northern Central collided head-on, resulting in the deaths of twenty-nine persons and serious injury to dozens more. An excursion train was returning to the city carrying some of the 5,000 Independence Day celebrants who had spent the day at Rider's Grove (a popular local picnic area) when it collided with the "accommodation" train on its way to York.

The *Baltimore Sun* for Thursday July 6, 1854, gave a full account with five of the seven front-page columns dedicated to coverage of the tragedy. Vivid and poignant descriptions of the injuries in excruciating detail related how many of these poor unsuspecting souls met their untimely deaths.

> One of the most terrible and appalling railroad accidents ever witnessed in this country has taken place on the Baltimore and Susquehanna Railroad at a point 9 miles from the city, about midway between Rider's Grove and the Relay House.
>
> When the collision occurred the crash was of a most terrific character, the locomotive of the outward train and the cars of the other being smashed beyond repair, whilst the groans of the dying, the heart rendering shrieks of the wounded, as well as the mangled bodies of the dead, presented a scene which defied faithful description.
>
> Three were instantly killed on the front platform of the York train, one of whom was Benjamin Merryman, the baggage master, who met death standing manfully at his post endeavoring to check the destruction.
>
> About 800-1000 walked all the way to the city from the grove a distance of nine miles including many females and children who

THE SUN.

VOL. XXXV.—NO. 42.]   BALTIMORE, THURSDAY MORNING, JULY 6, 1854.   [PRICE ONE CENT.

[Reported for the Baltimore Sun.]

DREADFUL
RAILROAD ACCIDENT.
AWFUL LOSS OF LIFE.
28 PERSONS KILLED.
Fifty or Sixty Persons Wounded.

NAMES OF THE KILLED AND WOUNDED.

Incidents, Funerals, Coroners' Inquests, &c.

One of the most terrible and appalling railroad accidents ever witnessed in this country has taken place on the Baltimore and Susquehanna railroad at a point 9 miles from the city, about midway between Rider's Grove and the Relay House.

It appears that on Tuesday afternoon the regular accommodation train for York, consisting of 5 large 8 wheeled passenger cars left the Calvert station at 25 minutes past 4 o'clock, containing about two hundred persons, in charge of Mr. Wm. D. Scott, conductor, accompanied by Mr. R. S. Hollins, the treasurer, and other officers of the road, who proceeded out for the purpose of assisting in the management of the return trains from Rider's Grove, where nearly three thousand persons had been conveyed by the company for the purpose of celebrating the day. This large party of men, women and children, had gone out during the morning in three different trains.

The accommodation train, above referred to, proceeded out carefully at a moderate rate of speed until it reached the Relay House, where it was duly switched off on the Green Spring branch, in order to let the down trains pass.

The express train due in Baltimore at 12 o'clock noon then passed along, having been detained; also an excursion train from Rider's woods, which consisted of nineteen large cars, all crowded with the excursionists, on their return home.

The accommodation train then proceeded, but had not traveled a mile before it came in collision with the second excursion train from Rider's Grove, consisting of fourteen cars filled with men, women and children, in charge of Mr. Jno. Scott, one of the most experienced conductors on the road. When the collision occurred the crash was of a most terrific character, the locomotive of the outward train, and the cars of the other being smashed beyond repair, whilst the groans of the dying, the heart-rending shrieks of the wounded, suffered much from heat and dust but truly thankful that they had escaped with their lives and without broken limbs.

After the catastrophe, an aged gentleman was observed standing near the body of Mrs. Robinson in a most distressed state of mind, indulging in unavailing accusations against himself for having persuaded her to accompany the excursion.[4]

Neighborhood residents were quick to respond to the tragedy. George McConkey sheltered several of the injured, including the train conductor, John Scott. W. J. McDaniel (Hopyard) supplied water and linens for bandages. Both were recognized in the *Sun* account.

In reporting the accident to shareholders, the 1854 annual report for the railroad (year ending September 30, two months after the wreck) related the following:

> This deplorable accident excited the warmest feelings of sympathy in the Directors for the wounded and for the families and friends of the deceased, and prompt measures were adopted to relieve as far as possible their wants, and to alleviate their sufferings. Everything was done that was in their power to accomplish; and we feel gratified in being able to say that nearly all of the claims for damages which have grown out of this collision have been satisfactorily adjusted.[5]

American society was less litigious in 1854 than today. It is difficult to imagine the railroad surviving the lawsuits that would have been filed had it been the 1990s.

The calamity that struck the Ruxton community on an otherwise peaceful and routine holiday afternoon helped play a role in the future of transportation regulation. In an understandable reaction to the flagrant disregard for even the most elementary safety and operating procedures in this incident and others, public opinion gradually began to build for government action that culminated in the reform legislation of the Progressive era several decades later. In addition, the development of mechanical and magnetic technologies for rail-

Opposite. Safety standards and devices failed to keep pace with the dangers associated with popular travel by rail in the 1850s. In its edition of July 6, 1854, the *Baltimore Sun* reported the rail tragedy at Ruxton on Independence Day. *(Special Collections Library, University of Maryland-Baltimore County.)*

road scheduling, communication, and management contributed greatly to answering the public's demand for safer travel standards.

On a lighter note, the community took pride in playing host, even if only for a moment, to one of the most famous personalities in American history. On the morning of November 16, 1863, President Abraham Lincoln traveled the Northern Central on his way to the dedication of the Gettysburg National Cemetery and again on his return to Washington the next day. He was accompanied on the special train by Secretary of State William H. Seward, Secretary of the Interior John P. Usher, and John W. Garrett and J. D. Cameron presidents of the Baltimore & Ohio and Northern Central, respectively.[6]

The *Sun* reported that during the journey the President frequently appeared on the rear platform to acknowledge the greetings of citizens who had gathered along the tracks. Whether he was moved to do so when the train passed through the Roland Run Valley cannot be ascertained. His attention most assuredly was drawn to the newly completed Lake Roland reservoir and to the site of the train wreck nine years earlier. Regrettably, the next time Lincoln traveled the Northern Central it was on his funeral train headed for Harrisburg and the trip back to Springfield, Illinois.

Despite its unpopular beginnings, the railroad has been accepted affectionately as part of the neighborhood's colorful past even though its impact diminished steadily after 1900. If the railroad had never been built and Ruxton had grown up without it, one can only imagine the public outcry if suddenly one of the major railroads announced plans to cut the area in two. With today's light rail system we now witness this 150-year-old asset once again returned to public use. Unfortunately, some current residents are no more pleased with the new rail system than their forebears were with the old.

Afterword

———————

Nothing of any great significance occurred in Ruxton, we might say, yet all local histories have their own uniqueness and importance, for no two are exactly alike. Unfortunately, history seldom records the happenings of the "average" citizen, but in the aggregate it is the economic, social, and political forces such people create that act as catalyst for greater events. The study of how ordinary people develop their culture gives local history its real dynamic, but it is also easily forgotten. Recent recognition of this has driven an increased interest and credibility in the study of local history, formerly reserved for neighborhood folklorists.

Local history can be relevant to contemporary life. The rich research resources that bring these ancestors to life serve our curiosity by providing us with knowledge and appreciation of the lives they lived and a key to who we are today. An orderly and disciplined way of life was established through strong religious values and a passion for independence, but mutual interdependence when required. They developed a common work ethic, a drive to improve their lot from generation to generation, and a belief in democratic ideals that continue to serve us well.

Several conclusions can be drawn from this review of Ruxton's early history. First, students of Maryland history are fortunate in having a wide variety of local and primary research resources available from which to open a window to the past. These detailed and well organized records were created out of recognition, under the traditions of English common law, of the need to establish property rights firmly. Confidence in provincial government's ability to maintain order and guarantee the succession of this property system has been essential in ensuring public support and perpetuation.

Our study of Ruxton shows the growth and transformation of the middling planter from a force of stability, power, and the status quo during the colonial period to what later became a force of revolution when economic and personal freedom became restricted or denied. This powerful force led to a new nation seeking to be free of past loyalties, prohibitions, and prejudices. The revolutionaries of this period, unlike those of today in so many parts of the world, had everything to lose yet they were willing to take that risk.

The challenge of settling, distributing, and administering vast areas of wilderness, without any precedent to be guided by or any of the modern administrative tools we enjoy today, was truly a mammoth undertaking involving great courage, confidence, and patience. This was economic development in its pure and original state.

The historic record presented here, drawn from archival resources that are available to all, provides miniature biographies of early settlers, any of which can be more fully developed. As we reveal and recognize their individual contributions, we also discover the aggregate impact of their efforts on our society today. Their success laid the early foundations of capital surplus, capital investment, and capital improvement that led to Maryland's contribution to colonial development, the Industrial Revolution, and later to the United States as a world power.

Notes

————◆————

This study of early Ruxton is based largely on land, will (inventory), and tax records that are readily available to researchers at the Maryland State Archives (MSA), also known as the Maryland Hall of Records, in Annapolis, and the Baltimore County Courthouse in Towson. Records prior to 1856 are located at MSA; later records are in Towson. In the notes that follow Baltimore County is abbreviated BC; Baltimore County Lands Records, BCLR.

INTRODUCTION

1. Land, Aubrey C., "Planters of Colonial Maryland," *Maryland Historical Magazine* 67, no. 2 (1972): 111.
2. Ibid., 109–128; Neal Brooks and Eric Rochel, *A History of Baltimore County* (Towson, Md.: Friends of the Towson Library, 1979), 11–24.
3. Suzanne E. G. Chapelle, Jean H. Baker, Dean R. Esslinger, Whitman H. Ridgway, Jean B. Russo, Constance B. Schultz, and Gregory A. Stiverson, *Maryland: A History of Its People* (Baltimore: Johns Hopkins University Press, 1986), 34.

1. SAMUEL'S HOPE

1. BC Land Patents, C No. 3/273.
2. Hooker Family Chart by Wilson Mile Cary, Maryland Historical Society, Baltimore.
3. BCLR, TR, no. A/452.
4. BCLR, TR, no. A/528 (1718).
5. BCLR, TR, no. DS/277 (1720).
6. BCLR, IS, no. IK/313.
7. BC Wills, 22/477.
8. BC Inventories, 27/163; Edward Wright, *Inhabitants of Baltimore Co. 1692–1763* (Silver Spring, Md.: Family Line Publications, 1987), 20.
9. BC Court Proceedings, HWS, No. IA/Z.
10. Marriage File, Maryland Historical Society.
11. BC Wills, 3/142.
12. BC Inventories, 11/1-4.
13. *Leading Families of Baltimore City and County* (New York: Chapman Publishing Co., 1897), 300.
14. Henry Peden, *Revolutionary Patriots of Baltimore Town and Baltimore County, Maryland, 1775–1783* (Silver Spring, Md.: Family Line Publications, 1988), 26.
15. *First Census of the United States, 1790* (Baltimore: Maryland Genealogical Publishing Co., 1972), 23.
16. Federal Direct Tax (Maryland State Papers), 1798, Back River-Middle River Upper Hundreds, MSA S37.
17. BC Assessment of 1804, Back River-Upper Hundred, MSA C277, 53.
18. BC Wills, 7/444–447, MSA 11, 616.
19. BCLR, WG, no. 144/339–340.

20. BC Wills, 3/138.
21. BC Inventories, 11/60.
22. BC Court [Tax List], 1773, Back River-Upper Hundred, MSA C428.
23. BC Wills, 9/70.
24. BC Inventories, WB, no. 26/556–560.
25. BCLR, WG, no.137/237.
26. BCLR, TR, no. D/432.
27. BC Wills, 7/293.
28. BCLR, WG, no. 54/675.
29. F. Edward Wright, *Maryland Militia War of 1812*, vol. 2 (Silver Spring Md.: Family Line Publications, 1979), 75.
30. A. K. Gilbert, "Gunpowder Production In Post Revolutionary Maryland," *Maryland Historical Magazine* 52, no. 3 (1957), 193–195.
31. BCLR, AI, no. 221/16–17.
32. BC Wills, 14/403.
33. BC Inventories, 43/135.
34. BCLR, MHF, no.3/157.

35. *Baltimore County Advocate*, August 7, 1852.
36. BCLR, MHF, no. 6/359.
37. BCLR: GHC, 30/330; GHC, 34/121; GHC, 31/103; HMF, 6/359; GHC, 24/14; HMF. 20/294; GHC, 39/365; MHF, 17/108; BC Judicial Record, EHA, no. 29/73.
38. BCLR, HMF, no. 20/294.
39. Inventory Site Survey, BA–929, January 1979, Maryland Historical Trust, Crownsville Md.
40. William Hollifield, *Difficulties Made Easy: History of the Turnpikes of Baltimore City and County* (Cockeysville Md.: Baltimore County Historical Society), 240.
41. BC Wills 5/240
42. *Leading Families of Baltimore City and County*, 278–279.
43. Edward C. Papenfuse and Joseph M. Coale III, *Atlas of Historic Maps of Maryland 1608 – 1908* (Baltimore: Johns Hopkins University Press, 1982), 107.

2. Hector's Hopyard

1. BC Land Patent, Liber C, no. 3, Folio 69.
2. CLR, HW, no. 2/132.
3. BC Wills, 19/791–799.
4. BCLR, TB, no. A/184–185.
5. BC Land Grant, no. p.t., no. 2/323.
6. BC Unpatented Certificate of Survey, no. 1788 (1750).
7. BCLR, TB, no. E/532; TR, no. D/224R; AL, no. A/606R.
8. BC Wills, 3/464–466; BC Inventory, 12/418.
9. Assessment Record, 1783, Maryland General Assembly, MSA S1161.
10. Federal Direct tax, 1798, Maryland. State Papers, MSA S37.
11. Federal Census, 1790.
12. BC Wills, 8/310–311.
13. BCLR, WG, no.68/498.
14. Ibid.; BCLR: WG, no. 79/341; WG, no. 120/443; WG, no. 143/91; WG, no. 153/253; BC Court Records, WG 4:67.
15. BCLR: WG, no. 79/346–348; WG, no. 68/502.
16. BC Circuit Court Records, Book WG, no.4:67.
17. BCLR, IS, no. IK/255–258.
18. BC Wills, no. 1/92–93; Thomas, ibid, 68–71.
19. D. F. Thomas, *The Green Spring Valley: Its History and Heritage* (Baltimore: Maryland Historical Society, 1978), 68-71.
20. BC Wills, no. 3/107–8.
21. BCLR, WG, no. D/194–195.
22. Ibid., WG, no. 58/609–611.
23. *Baltimore American*, May 10, 1811.
24. BCLR, WG, no. 116/455 (Chancery L 78 F 146). The site map of the mill works was discovered during a search of the records pertaining to the case and has been preserved by MSA.
25. Ibid., WG, no. 147/226.
26. BC Wills, WBL 12/84.
27. BCWT, 96054–12055, National Archives, Washington DC.
28. BCLR, TK, no. 232/222.
29. Ibid., HMF, no. 10/505.
30. Ibid., HMF, no. 16/438.
31. BC Judicial Records, EHA, no. 29/130.
32. BCLR, HMF, no. 48/14; HMF, no. 48/17.
33. J. Thomas Scharf, *History of Baltimore City and County* (1881; rep. Baltimore: Regional Publishing Co., 1971), 71.
34. C. Colman Hall, *History of Baltimore 1730–1797* (Baltimore: Lewis Historical

Publishing Co., 1912), 28.

35. Gilbert, "Gunpowder Production," 193–195.

36. William Kilty, *The Laws of Maryland From the End of the Year 1799*, vol. 5 (Annapolis: J. Green, 1818), chapter 78.

37. Gilbert, "Gunpowder Production," 193.

38. United States War Department, Letters Sent, Record Group no.156, National Archives, Washington DC.

39. *Baltimore News-Post*, May 17, 1945.

40. *American Commercial and Daily Advisor*, August 30, 1820.

41. Gilbert, "Gunpowder Production," 194.

42. BC Chancery Court, 1831: MSA 6623; MSA 6623. See also BCLR AI, no. 221/23.

43. *Site Map of Powdermills*, Hagley Museum and Library, Wilmington, Del., 82.285.1.

44. BCLR, AI, no. 221/23.

45. *Baltimore Sun*, October 7, 1851.

46. BCLR, HMF, no. 5/254.

47. *Baltimore News-Post*, May 17, 1941.

3. Bosley's Adventure

1. BC Patented Certificate of Survey, no. 721.

2. BC Wills, 3/213.

3. BC Wills 3/330; BC Administrative Accounts, no. 7/358.

4. BC Inventories, 11/322–330.

5. BC Chancery Court Record, no. 3836 (1796).

6. BCLR, WG, no. E/519.

7. Ibid., WG, no. H/379–381.

8. Ibid., WG, no. Z/362.

9. Ibid., WG, no. DD/335–336.

10. Ibid., WG, no.GG/557; no. DD/333.

11. Ibid., WG, no. 140/34–37.

12. Ibid., WG, no. 149/183.

13. Ibid, WG, no. QQ/468.

14. For a fuller account of Moore's life see Edward Steiner, "Nicholas Ruxton Moore: Soldier, Farmer and Politician," *Maryland Historical Magazine 73*, no. 4 (1978), 375–384; see also Scharf, History, 78-98.

15. BCLR, HMF, no. 10/505.

16. BC Chancery Court Papers, 1819/05/27, Box C,518 (602-001-431); MSA. 40,200–126 2/15/11/35.

17. *American Commercial and Daily Advisor*, August 8, 1821.

18. BCLR, WG, no. 71/9-13.

19. Ibid., AWB, no. 437/51.

20. Ibid., HMF, no. 10/412.

21. Ibid., GHC, no. 25/312.

22. Ibid., JWS, no. 153/122.

23. *Baltimore Sun*, February 7, 1887.

4. Young Man's Adventure

1. BC Patent CD f.f. 133–134.

2. BLCR, TR, no. A 108–110.

3. BC Wills, no. 14/62.

4. BCLR, TB, no. A Folio 22–25.

5. BC Certificate, no. 1123.

6. BC Certificate, no. 1121.

7. BC Prerogative Court (Wills), no. 31, 524–526.

8. BC Wills, 8/494 (new 465).

9. BC Inventories, 26/198 (1809).

10. BC Patented Land Certificate, no. 5399.

11. BC Wills, 17/170; BC Inventory, 55/366.

12. Philemon Coale family Bible entries (collection of the author); W.H. Burgan, *History of Hunt's Church* (privately published, 1910), 15; Edward Wright, *Maryland Militia War of 1812*, vol. 2 (Silver Spring, Md.: Family Line Publications, 1979), 74-75; BCWT 4700-160-55, National Archives, Washington, D.C.; BCLR, TK, no. 231/53,221/13; BLCR, TK, 265/529. 160-55; BCLR, no. TK 231/53, 221/13 e; BCLR, no. TK 265/529.

13. *Baltimore Sun*, November 13, 1845.

14. BCLR, AWB, no. 381/284.

15. Ibid., HMF, no. 14/54.

16. Ibid., no. 25/312.

17. *Leading Families*, 172.

18. BC Plat Book, JWS, no 1, filed September 14,1894.

5. Martinton and Martin's Addition

1. BC Land Patents: CD, no. 167; DD, no. 5/202; PC, no. 2/99.
2. BCLR, TR, no. A/108-110.
3. BC Wills, 14/6.
4. BCLR, TB, no.A/22-25.
5. BC Land Patent, no. 1123.
6. BCLR, TB, no. C/249.
7. Ibid., WG, no. F/90.
8. Edward Papenfuse, et al, *Biographical Dictionary of the Maryland Legislature 1635–1789*, vol. 2 (Baltimore: Johns Hopkins University Press, 1985), 686.
9. Papenfuse and Coale, *Atlas of Historic Maps*, 51.
10. BC Wills, WB, no. 1/150.
11. BCLR, WG, no. EE/208.
12. BC Wills, 8/242–243.
13. BC Wills, 10/284.
14. BCLR, WG, no. 121/275; WG, no. 123/265.
15. Ibid., WG, no. 158/626–629.
16. BC unpatented certificate of survey, no. 604, 1776, MSA S1213.
17. BCLR, WG, no. 186/175.
18. Ibid., WG, no. 212/589.
19. Ibid., TK, no. 231/53.

6. Hooker's Prosperity

1. BC Land Patents: no. 2/241; D.D., no.5/48.
2. BC Wills, 1/299.
3. BC Inventories, 23/437.
4. Brooks and Rochel, *History of Baltimore County*, 68-69.
5. BC Wills, 4/204.
6. BC Inventories, 14/312.
7. Burgan, *Hunt's Church*, 4.
8. *Baltimore County Union News*, February 7, 1914.
9. BCLR, WG 56/384.
11. BC Wills, DMP 13/153.
12. BCLR, 69/247.
13. Ibid., 68/127 (1872); 76/502 (1871). See also Scharf, *History*, 390.

7. Beale's Discovery

1. Thomas, *The Green Spring Valley*, 45-48, 168-173
2. BCLR Certificate, DD, no. 5, 125 Patent CD, no. 60–61.
3. Ibid., IS, no. L/273.
4. Ibid., TB, no. C/416–418; EI, no. 3/460–464.
5. BC Wills, 23/375–379.
6. BCLR, B, no. O/175–177.
7. Ibid., B, no. O/693–695.
8. Ibid., B, no. P/290.
9. Ibid., AL, no. B/350–352.
10. BC Wills, 3/217–218.
11. BCLR, AL, no. G/505–513.
12. Ibid., WG, no. Z/295–6.
13. BC Wills, 8/381.
14. BCLR, WG, no. 124/374.
15. BC Chancery Records filed March 28, 1814, MSA 17, 898–2241.
16. BCLR, WG, no. 184/78.
17. Burgan, *Hunt's Church*, 10.
18. BC Wills, 16/215–218.
19. Burgan, *Hunt's Church*, 11.

8. The Baltimore & Susquehanna Railroad

1. Scharf, *History*, 342–348.
2. BCLR: TK 254/532, 265/529, 268/521; AI 221/7,10,13,16,17.
3. Scharf, *History*, 344.
4. *Baltimore Sun*, July 6,1854.
5. Twenty–Seventh Annual Report of the President and Directors of the Baltimore & Susquehanna Railroad Company (Baltimore: James Lucas and Sons, 1854), 11–12.
6. *Baltimore Sun*, November 19, 1863.

Index

81

ABOUT THE AUTHOR

JOSEPH M. COALE III was born and raised in Baltimore. He is a graduate of Washington College in Chestertown and holds a master's degree in public administration from the University of Baltimore. He is Director of Corporate Communications and Public Affairs at Crown Central Petroleum Corporation. A dedicated amateur historian, he is co-author (with Maryland State Archivist Edward C. Papenfuse) of the *Hammond-Harwood Atlas of Historical Maps of Maryland, 1698-1908*. Mr. Coale lives in Ruxton with his wife Kim and their two sons, Robert and Benjamin.

Designed by Gerard A. Valerio,
Bookmark Studio, Annapolis, Maryland

Composed in Caslon by Sherri Armstrong,
Typeline, Annapolis

Printed on Mohawk Superfine by
Thomson-Shore, Inc., Dexter, Michigan

PART OF
3RD 8TH & 9TH
DISTRICTS
Reproduced in 1983
by The Friends of the Towson Library from the 1898
Bromley Atlas of Baltimore County

(16)